NEW LEFT REVIEW 28

SECOND SERIES

JULY AUGUST 2004

PROGRAMME NOTES

Susan Watkins: Vichy on the Tigris

With the now unanimous support of the 'international community', can Washington hope to recoup its gamble in Iraq? Prospects for the resistance and the Occupation, as the UN-approved government is hoisted into place.

'Alliance for Ethnic Equality': Tensions in Taiwan

Taiwanese artists, activists and intellectuals organize against the fanning of ethnic differences by DPP Greens and KMT Blues during the island's 2004 election. Cultural identity and official 'de-Sinicization' in a fast-expanding East Asian context.

Franco Moretti: Graphs, Maps, Trees—3

After 'graphs' and 'maps', trees: can evolutionary theory help pattern the transformation of cultural forms and divergence of genres, through time and space? Franco Moretti's final essay on abstract models for literary history.

Çağlar Keyder: The Turkish Bell Jar

Against a background of high unemployment and fragile economic recovery, the neo-Islamist AKP is submitting its supporters among the urban poor to the programmes of the IMF, Pentagon and Kemalist elite. Internal pressures on NATO's Middle East bridgehead and EU candidate member.

BENEDICT ANDERSON: Rizal's Worlds

After the literary revelations of 'Nitroglycerine in the Pomegranate' (NLR 27), a new political reading of José Rizal's astonishing last novel. Imperial power, anarchist bombings and anti-colonial insurrection in the gifted young Filipino's vision of a 19th-century global landscape.

BOOK REVIEWS

ARIF DIRLIK on Chaohua Wang, *One China, Many Paths*. A collective magnifying glass on the PRC's complex social and political problems, as some of the country's leading critical intellectuals debate its future.

RACHEL MALIK on Alex Woloch, *The One vs the Many*. The creation of character-systems in the realist novel, in a bold account that proposes a new political economy of major and minor.

JACOB STEVENS on Gareth Stedman Jones, Introduction to *The Communist Manifesto*. Intellectual antecedents of the trumpet blast of 1848. Must today's critics lower their political horizons?

CONTRIBUTORS

BENEDICT ANDERSON: *author of* Imagined Communities *(1983)*
and The Spectre of Comparisons *(1998); see also* NLR 27

CHU TIEN-HSIN: *her novellas, including* Le Dernier Train Pour
Tamsui *(1984) have just been published in a collection with her
father's and sister's work, translated as* Anthologie de la
famille Chu *(2004)*

ARIF DIRLIK: *teaches Chinese and cultural studies at the University
of Oregon; co-author of* Chinese on the American Frontier *(2003)*

HOU HSIAO-HSIEN: *director of over 15 films including* The City of
Sadness *(1989) and* The Puppet Master *(1993), his latest is*
Coffee Time *(2004)*

HSIA CHU-JOE: *teaches architecture and planning at the National
Taiwan University; founding editor of* Chengshi Yushegui
[Cities and Design]

ÇAĞLAR KEYDER: *teaches sociology at Boğaziçi University and* SUNY
Binghamton; editor of *Istanbul: Between the Global
and the Local *(1999)*

RACHEL MALIK: *teaches English at Middlesex University*

FRANCO MORETTI: *teaches literature at Stanford;* Atlas of the
European Novel *appeared in 1998; see also* NLR 24 and 26

TANG NUO: *Taiwanese writer and critic, expert in detective fiction;
his latest book is on the etymology of Chinese ideograms* (2002)

SUSAN WATKINS

Editorial

VICHY ON THE TIGRIS

His Majesty's Government and I are in the same boat and must sink or swim together . . . if you wish me and your policy to succeed, it is folly to damn me permanently in the public eye by making me an obvious puppet.

> *King Faisal I to the British High Commissioner,*
> *Mesopotamia, 17 August 1921.*[1]

ARELY HAS A passage of powers been so furtive. The ceremony—held two days ahead of schedule, deep within Baghdad's fortified Green Zone—lasted just ten minutes, with thirty US and Iraqi officials present. Outside the cement stockade, the military realities remain the same: an Occupation force of 160,000 US-led troops, an additional army of commercial security guards, and jumpy local police units. Before departing, the Coalition Provisional Authority set in place a parallel government structure of Commissioners and Inspectors-General (still referring to themselves as 'coalition officials' a week after the supposed dissolution of that body) who, elections notwithstanding, will control Iraq's chief ministries for the next five years.[2] The largest US embassy in the world will dominate Baghdad, with regional 'hubs' planned in Mosul, Kirkuk, Hilla and Basra. Most of the $3.2 billion that has been contracted so far is going on the construction of foreign military bases.[3] The UN has resolved that the country's oil revenues will continue to be deposited in the US-dominated Development Fund for Iraq, again for the next five years. The newly installed Allawi government will have no authority to reallocate contracts signed by the CPA, largely with foreign companies who will remain above the law of the land. Two thirds of the cabinet ministers are themselves US or UK citizens.

Iyad Allawi, hailed in the Western media as the blunt, independent-minded leader the country needs, is an appropriate appointment as prime minister. Little secret is made of the fact that, like his counterpart Karzai in Afghanistan, he has been a paid CIA agent for many years; the time is long past when that was considered something to hide. Allawi's career to date has more than qualified him for his present role. Iraqis recall him as a Baath enforcer in London student circles of the 1970s, with a bogus medical degree conferred by the regime for services rendered. According to an ex-INA colleague, he was simultaneously dealing with MI6 and running a Mukhabarat death squad for Saddam's faction, targeting Baath dissenters in Europe, until falling foul of it himself in 1978.[4] After a few years in hiding he resurfaced in Amman, co-founding the Iraqi National Accord in 1991 with Salih Omar Ali al-Tikriti, a former supervisor of public hangings in Baghdad. The INA specialized in recruiting military and intelligence defectors; the bomb blasts attributed to it in the mid-90s—one in a crowded theatre, another killing schoolchildren on a bus—were purportedly 'proficiency tests', set by the CIA. Duly persuaded of the INA's merits, the Agency provided funding for Allawi's botched coup attempt of 1996 which, uncovered by Saddam, resulted in over a hundred executions. He was subsequently responsible for passing on the intelligence that prompted Blair's claim of 45-minute WMD delivery systems, and pinpointed Saddam's supposed bunker for bombardment at the start of the 2003 Iraq War.[5]

With the Occupation in place, Allawi was put on the Governing Council in charge of security. His campaign for the post of prime minister—his lobbying firm spent over $370,000—was naturally run in Washington,

---

[1] Telegram from the High Commissioner, Mesopotamia, to the Secretary of State for the Colonies. The British had been concerned lest King Faisal 'did not realize what degree of control we expect him to submit to'. Hanna Batatu, *The Old Social Classes and the Revolutionary Movements of Iraq* [1978], London 2004. p. 324. Many thanks to Sami Ramadani and others for their comments and observations. They naturally bear no responsibility for what follows.
[2] A CPA-appointed official on the Communications and Media Commission in charge of media licensing explained that 'they can kiss goodbye to any European funds' and 'considerable US resources would be withheld' if there were any attempt by the interim minister to disobey the Commission. *Financial Times*, 5 July 2004.
[3] *Economist*, 26 June 2004; *Financial Times*, 5 July 2004.
[4] For former INA propagandist Dirgam Kadhim's account: Eli Lake, *New York Sun*, 17 January 2004; Seymour Hersh, 'Plan B', *New Yorker*, 28 June 2004.
[5] *Daily Telegraph*, 7 December 2003.

not Baghdad.[6] Once appointed, he embarrassed his masters by attempting to proclaim martial law before his inauguration. His colleague Ghazi al-Yawar, Iraq's new president, made a comparable show of independence by demurring from Bush's proposal to blow up Abu Ghraib: it would be a pity to demolish the prison when the Americans had spent so much money on it. (Yawar, an obscure telecoms manager in Saudi Arabia when the US established contact with him not long before the invasion, began dressing up in Shammar tribal robes as soon as he was put on the Governing Council; perhaps a tip from Karzai in Afghanistan.) Similarly, the first act of the interim Human Rights minister, Bakhtiyar Amin, was to announce state-of-emergency legislation. His predecessor on the Human Rights portfolio, a fellow Kurd, had resigned in disgust at the torture photographs from Abu Ghraib; Amin has showed no such compunction.

Character of the resistance

That it has taken Washington over a year to establish such a threadbare front—Karzai was parachuted into place in Kabul within a matter of days—is testimony to the strength of the resistance. In June 1940 the French Army, like its modern Iraqi counterpart, collapsed in face of the German *Blitzkrieg* without a serious fight. Within a month French National Assembly deputies gathered at Vichy had voted, 569 to 80, in favour of a collaborationist regime under Marshal Pétain.[7] The Vichy government was swiftly recognized by the US and other powers, and the majority of non-Jewish French settled down to life under the Occupation. It was two years before the *maquis* began to offer serious resistance. Elsewhere in Europe, the pattern was similar. The Germans were efficient in organizing indigenous support: Quisling in Norway, the Croatian Ustashi and ss-trained Bosnian and Kosovan regiments in Yugoslavia, Iron Cross in Romania, Arrow Cross in Hungary. In their classical form, twentieth-century resistance movements were slow to constitute themselves. Those that did appear nearly always had external

---

[6] For the sum Allawi's hired lobbyists Theros & Theros set up meetings with Bill Frist, Richard Lugar, Dennis Hastert, Tom DeLay, Henry Hyde, assorted National Security Council officials, VP's office, Defence Department and CIA, as well as getting Allawi a column in the *Washington Post*. See Ken Guggenheim, *Associated Press*, 24 January 2004; Jim Drinkard, USA Today, 2 June 2004.
[7] For the comparison, see Tariq Ali, 'Postscript', in the paperback edition of *Bush in Babylon*, to be published by Verso in October 2004.

state support. If the Allies' supplies were crucial to the anti-Nazi underground of Continental Europe, the general pattern was much the same in Asia or Africa. Chinese weaponry was a condition of Vietminh victory, as Egyptian and Tunisian backing was for the FLN in Algeria. Typically, such foreign help functioned in conjunction with an already existing political leadership and party network with a potential for hegemony at national level, as with the local Communist movements in France, Italy or Indochina.

The resistance that has emerged over the past year to the US Occupation in Iraq fits none of these categories. It began early, the first armed attacks erupting in May 2003, within weeks of Baghdad's fall. It escalated over the summer, as demonstrations and street protests were regularly fired upon. ('The apprentice is gone, the master is here' was the chant of the million-strong march on Karbala that spring.) The initial hit-and-miss harrying of the Occupation force—roadside devices, rocket-propelled missiles, amateurish shelling of the CPA compound—had developed by August 2003 into assaults on strategic military and diplomatic targets: the Jordanian Embassy, the UN compound. By November US forces were suffering heavier losses, with the insurgents bringing down helicopters. Vicious reprisals led to a further escalating spiral. Like any other military occupation, the Anglo-American regime has been one of sanctioned murder and torture; the resistance to it has been savage, too.[8] Suicide raids, car bombs and mortars have sown havoc in the big cities. Attacks on US forces doubled between October and December 2003, from around fifteen to over thirty; by June 2004 they had risen to an estimated forty-five a day. Increasingly sophisticated assaults on pipelines and pumping-stations (estimated at over 2,000 in the past year) have cut oil exports for weeks at a time. Yet the simultaneous rebellions that broke out across the Shia south and Sunni centre in April 2004, and the joint Shia–Sunni convoy from Baghdad to Falluja, have done most to trigger the alarm of Western and Arab governments—prefiguring a national resistance leadership, to be avoided at all costs. Meanwhile, CPA polls measured the solid bank of popular support behind the fighters: some 92 per cent of Iraqis saw the US troops as occupiers; only 2 per cent considered them a liberation force.

---

[8] For a vivid portrayal of the mindset of alienated US troops—a cocktail of gun culture, video games, pornography and deracinated violence—see Evan Wright, *Generation Kill*, New York 2004; the prevalence in US prisons of the methods of humiliation practised in Abu Ghraib has been well documented.

Nor has the Iraqi resistance received support from any foreign state. Externally, it faces a front of unprecedented official hostility—a global unanimity unimaginable in any previous age. UN Security Council resolution 1546, passed on 8 June 2004, extends unqualified support to the CPA-appointed regime, conferring the full legitimacy of the 'international community' on its collection of old CIA hands and carpet-baggers.[9] Explaining that the country—lacking an army, and with a transparent absence of WMD—'continues to constitute a threat to international peace and security', it authorizes the US-led occupying force to take 'all necessary measures', ie, whatever American commanders deem fit. All UN members are, of course, bluntly prohibited from supplying arms or material to the Iraqi people. France and Germany offered the comedy of a request that sovereign control over the Occupier's army be entrusted to the Iraqi façade it has manufactured—only be told by Allawi and Yawar that Paris and Bonn should 'not be more Iraqi than the Iraqis', who desired only that the US command 'keep them informed'.

In the Middle East itself, the Arab states have played their accustomed role. The governments that rallied to Washington in the first Gulf War—Cairo, Damascus, Riyadh, Tunis, Algiers, Rabat—have stuck with it through the second, with Amman now rapidly catching up. Algeria voted for resolution 1546, Syria for its predecessor 1511 in October 2003. Mubarak has offered the services of Egypt's security services to train the new Iraqi *gendarmerie*, while simultaneously backing Israel's *razzias* in the Gaza strip. King Abdallah is providing parade grounds in Jordan and has readied his troops to help out. The wider Islamic world has proved equally reliable. In June the fifty-seven states of the Organization of the Islamic Conference met in Istanbul to pledge their support for the Occupation's native face—Karzai logically in the lead. Erdoğan, their host, has not only offered Turkish troops for Iraq but hurried to participate in Washington's Broader Middle East initiative, at which even Mubarak baulked. Iran has helped keep the southern clergy quiet as the Americans ring the shrine cities of the Shia heartland. In Pakistan, Musharraf is bombing his Waziri subjects on US instructions.

Politically, the Iraqi resistance has been heterogeneous and fragmentary, lacking the established party networks crucial to most previous

---

[9] Current UNSC members, in addition to the Permanent Five: Algeria, Angola, Benin, Brazil, Chile, Germany, Pakistan, Philippines, Romania, Spain.

anti-occupation movements. It includes Nasserites, former Baathists, secular liberals and social democrats, multi-hued mosque-based networks,
and splits from the collaborationist Iraqi Communist and Dawa parties.
American observers have commented on the social breadth of an opposition that draws on support from nearly every class, both urban and rural:
'Its ranks include students, intellectuals, former soldiers, tribal youths,
farmers and Islamists'.[10] Ideologically, nationalism and islamism—'for
God and Iraq'—are potent calls, but there are elements of Third World
anti-imperialism and pan-Arabism too. It remains to be seen whether
these groups can establish some equivalent of a national liberation front,
to unite religious and secular groups around the central demand for the
expulsion of all foreign troops.

Subjective resources

Externally isolated and internally unsynchronized, the Iraqi *maquis* nevertheless possesses a number of distinct resources. First, strong social
networks: resilient clan and extended-family connexions; city neighbourhood quarters that retain some cohesion; mosques that offer a safe
local gathering place, unimaginable in occupied Europe. Arab writers
have pointed out the attendant weaknesses of these forms: particular-
ism, local rivalry, lack of coordination, the treachery or opportunism of
unaccountable demagogues, a fringe of criminality—though within this
fluid, oral and highly mobilized environment, leaders can also be forced
into taking more resolute stands, to retain their supporters.[11]

Second, the considerable quantity of arms that the resistance has at its
disposal. American estimates—three million tons of bombs and bul-
lets, AK47s, rocket launchers and mortar tubes, plus the artillery shells
used to make roadside bombs—may be inflated. But unlike previous
anti-occupation movements, plagued by lack of arms, it seems likely that
the Iraqi guerrillas have sufficient explosives to harry the occupiers for
years to come. Shock-resistant, these weapons have to be painstakingly
dismantled, one by one; an attempt to blow up an ammunitions stack

---

[10] Ahmed Hashim, 'Terrorism and Complex Warfare in Iraq', Jamestown Foundation,
18 June 2004.
[11] Points made in the last essays of the novelist Abderrahman Munif (1933–2004),
published as *Al-Iraq: Hawamish min al-Tarikh wa al-Moquoumah* [Iraq: Footnotes
from History and Resistance], Beirut 2003.

simply scatters it, unexploded. The US has only a few hundred engineers in Iraq capable of the task.[12]

Third, the natural dislike of any people for a foreign occupation has been reinforced by the stark deterioration of social conditions since the Anglo-American invasion. In much of the countryside, the long-term agrarian crisis—salination, pump failure, silted canals—is worsening as agribusiness imports increase. Rising rural unemployment has swollen the slum populations of Basra and Baghdad. In most towns outside the North, small businesses have been hit by a combination of cheap foreign goods and the breakdown of law and order. Much of Iraq's shrunken 70s-era industrial sector—already skewed towards arms production during the Iran–Iraq war, then targeted by Western bombs in the 1990s—faces not privatization but closure, putting a once-skilled workforce on the street. Two-thirds of the pre-invasion workforce may now be unemployed. As for the future, promotional literature for the country as a regional trade hub—a giant Dubai, handling freight operations for the Greater Middle East[13]—offers Iraqis little more than a distant prospect of integration into the global economy as baggage handlers and warehousemen. A deepening social crisis is concealed behind the daily military communiqués, and the tangible Occupation presence provides a ready target for its frustrations.

Fourthly, the resistance can draw upon vivid historical memories of battles finally won against the last imperial occupier. The modern Iraqi nation is a creation of the struggle against British colonialism, after London seized Mesopotamia from Istanbul in 1917. The countrywide uprising in the summer of 1920—small tribal sheikhs and sayyids along the Euphrates joining with ex-Ottoman officials in Baghdad and hard-hit northern merchants from Mosul—forced London to retreat from direct administration on the Delhi model. Its solution, 'ruling without governing' as the Secretary of State for the Colonies later defined it,[14] was to set up a monarchy dependent on British arms for survival, backed by a League of Nations Mandate authorizing 'all necessary measures'. The British High Commissioner remained the highest power in the land and, when

[12] Evan Wright, 'Iraq's vast arsenal', *International Herald Tribune*, 18 June 2004.
[13] See for example the effusions of Joseph Braude, *The New Iraq*, New York 2003, pp. 132–3.
[14] That is, 'exercising control through an ostensibly independent native government': L. S. Amery, Foreign Office Memorandum, 7 February 1929.

the Mandate expired, the Anglo-Iraqi Treaty guaranteed British control over Iraq's foreign policy, seaport, railways, airbases and, in times of war, security forces. Compliant local notables signed up to the Treaty, willing to forgo external independence—as one of them put it—as long as they had internal control. The majority of the population rejected it. When resistance broke out in 1922, the British High Commissioner arrested political leaders, banned nationalist parties and famously subdued rebellious tribes with punitive bombing and mustard gas.

But despite London's efforts to foster conservative landlordism in the countryside, packing tame national assemblies with loyal sheikhs and fabricating a 'manly' desert image for them, urban social forces could not be held down indefinitely. In 1936, social-democratic lawyers and civil servants joined forces with nationalist officers in a short-lived coup d'état. The nascent Iraqi Communist Party began organizing rank-and-file soldiers. Strike waves swept the Basra docks, Baghdad railway workshops, Najaf weaving factories, Kirkuk oil fields and Habbaniyah military base. In May 1941 the pro-British Regent, the Crown Prince and the Prime Minister Nuri al-Said were forced to flee abroad when pan-Arab officers with mass nationalist backing seized power and abrogated the wartime provisos of the Treaty. The UK had to re-occupy the country to restore imperial control, returning the Crown Prince to Baghdad in a British tank.

In January 1948 popular anger at the recycling of the Treaty[15] and at the British role in Palestine set off an insurrectionary movement in the capital, mingling middle-class students and nationalists with communist railway workers and slum-dwellers. In November 1952, another rising pitched them against Hashemite troops and police in the streets of Baghdad. Four years later riots erupted in Najaf and Hayy against the Anglo-French-Israeli attack on Egypt. Finally, in July 1958, a Free Officers' coup toppled the monarchy with the backing of both Communists and Baathists (at that time a small party with under a thousand members). Huge crowds clogged the streets to block any counter-revolution, as the Republic of Iraq was proclaimed by a left-nationalist government led by Abdul-Karim Qasim, and the door to national independence and social reform opened.[16]

[15] Now 'oiled over with the idioms of mutuality' in the form of the Portsmouth Agreement: Batatu, *Old Social Classes*, p. 550.
[16] It was the strength of the Iraqi Communists in this crucial Middle Eastern state that prompted the first, CIA-backed coup by the Baath Party, oil and business interests in 1963. For the US role as described by King Hussein of Jordan, see Batatu, *Old Social Classes*, pp. 985–6.

Iraqis are well tutored in these battles, the ABC of their modern history. But the past rarely offers exact analogies, and to view contemporary events through its lens highlights differences as well as similarities between the old imperial occupation and the new. Militarily and politically, the machinery of American power in Iraq today is far more formidable than Britain's was. With 160,000 troops at his disposal, Negroponte has a greater vice-regal command of violence than the British High Commissioner ever possessed. American control of Iraqi harbours, airports and security forces—not to speak of courts, education, trade, finance, media and foreign policy—has been given the UN seal, with a force of 'international law' going well beyond the bilateral Anglo-Iraqi Treaty. Washington's coffers are deeper than London's ever were, and today's oil revenues were undreamt of in the 1920s. The capacity of the Occupation to buy consent to its rule is far higher. It can also hope to rely on the sheer exhaustion and dislocation of life after March 2003 to create a desperate longing for some semblance of normalcy, under new arrangements that promise to transfer, however nominally, elements of sovereignty back to the country.

Prospects for the Green Zone

It would be a mistake therefore to think that nothing has changed since Bremer flew out of Iraq. As in the German-occupied Europe of 1940–41, native collaborationist regimes typically offer an initial degree of relief, after the humiliation of foreign invasion, as well as lucrative business or administrative positions to servants of the new order. The puppet government in Baghdad today enjoys far less autonomy than Pétain's regime in Vichy; in that respect it is closer to Quisling's in Oslo. But it has a basis of support from an array of privileged groups in the post-invasion landscape—not just carpet-baggers on CIA or MI6 payrolls but techno-crats, eyeing career opportunities; a large swathe of the semi-expatriate bourgeoisie and the sanction-busting *nouveaux riches*; traditionally collab-orationist rural families like the Yawars, leaders of the Shammar tribe in the Mosul region, who sided with the British in 1920; and the large Kurdish population in the North. For the moment, the regime also enjoys the toler-ance of the Shia hierarchy around Ayatollah Sistani; Tehran still seems bent on appeasing the US. Washington can hope at least to keep the situa-tion out of the news headlines in the run-up to the US elections. It may yet recoup its adventure with the stabilization of a client state—if the *maquis* can be crushed or co-opted before they sap too much domestic support.

All this, however, must contend with the general detestation of the Arab population for the American occupation itself. The foreign hand is everywhere visible in the new Iraq. Even in the North, where US troops are scarcely needed, the Kurdish leadership has installed a network of Israeli intelligence agents and hit squads, the culmination of its disastrous record of political misjudgements, if in a legitimate cause.[17] If its client regime is not to be permanently associated with American bombers, tanks and jails, the US urgently needs an effective native enforcement body.[18] It is one measure of the resistance's strength that, despite the unemployment levels, enlistments by June 2004 were lagging at 10 per cent of planned figures, and the loyalty of new recruits was still in doubt. It remains to be seen whether Allawi's attempts to brigade or buy over former Baath officers will produce better results.

On the ideological front there is little more light. The hazy electoral horizon already appears to be in doubt. Under rules endorsed by UN resolution 1546, the January 2005 polls (if they are held) will choose candidates selected by the US Embassy for a 'transitional' administration with strictly limited powers, charged with drafting a constitution for a further, equally restricted ballot by January 2006. In the meantime, a hand-picked, one-thousand-member consultative conference may or may not be called into being, to discuss appointing a smaller, equally consultative, body from amongst itself.[19]

Internationally, the regime and its masters look forward to strengthening their position by planting the UN flag once again in Iraqi soil. So far the

---

[17] The Pentagon has issued no denial of Seymour Hersh's detailed report in the *New Yorker* of Israel's qualitative expansion of its long-standing security foothold in Iraq's Kurdish provinces, training units of the 75,000 *peshmerga* in *mistaravim* commando tactics for operations in Iraq, Iran and Syria. According to a former Israeli intelligence officer, the Israeli leadership had concluded in August 2003 that, in terms of rescuing the situation in Iraq, 'It's over. Not militarily—the United States cannot be defeated militarily in Iraq—but politically'. 'Plan B' would attempt to salvage an independent Kurdistan, with access to Kirkuk's oil, as a strategic platform in the region. Hersh, *New Yorker*, 28 June 2004.
[18] Even if it wants it on the cheap. 'It is clear that a desire to reduce costs and cut corners was a big factor in the Pentagon's choice of Ukrainian gear . . . Dozens of US military suppliers revealed their disappointment at the minimal requirements': not even ballistic protection for troop carriers, or air-conditioning for ambulances. *Financial Times*, 18 June 2004.
[19] Elections for university deans held, as scheduled under the previous regime, in the summer of 2003 returned solidly anti-Occupation candidates; the CPA swiftly cancelled the mayoral polls due in their wake.

Secretariat has not dared to return to Baghdad—and with good reason. Infant mortality under the UN sanctions regime in the 1990s caused on conservative estimates some 300,000 deaths of childen under five from disease and malnutrition, while the Secretariat skimmed administration fees of over $1 billion. In December 1998 the UN contracts committee, working out of the Secretariat's office, awarded the 'oil for food' programme contract for monitoring Iraqi imports (of often rotted food and diluted medicines) to Cotecna Inspections, a company which employed Kofi Annan's son Kojo as a consultant throughout the bidding process.[20] In June special envoy Lakhdar Brahimi, a leading member of the junta that cancelled elections in Algeria in 1992, and broker of the Karzai regime in Afghanistan, rubber-stamped Bremer's selection of members of the Governing Council for reincarnation as ministers of the Interim Government; but, duty performed, could not wait to get out. When they do come back, UN functionaries will need a large private army of their own to protect them.

November and after

Formally speaking, the Anglo-American invasion has been stripped of its original pretexts. There were no weapons of mass destruction. Human-rights violations have branded the liberators. The need to bring democracy to Iraq, let alone the rest of the Middle East, has become less pressing. It is the strength of the Iraqi resistance—and it alone—that has led to widespread uneasiness in the Western establishments. Washington think tanks have begun to debate exit strategies, estimating the costs to US political credibility ('high, or unacceptable?'), assessing 'indicators for withdrawal'.[21] The American electorate has turned against

---

[20] Cotecna's undemanding task was to issue Confirmation of Arrival certificates for goods containers passing through Umm Qasr port or the Jordanian border crossing at Trebil, triggering payments from the UN escrow account into which the proceeds of Iraqi oil sales were paid. The UN contracts committee reports directly to the Secretary-General, who signed off on all the 6-monthly phases of the programme. The Secretariat is currently refusing to release details of Cotecna's fees to Congressional inquiries into the Kofigate scandal. In May 2003 the UNSC gave it six months to 'tie up loose ends' before administration of the oil funds switched to the CPA that November; in the process, 25 per cent of contracts were scrapped, as companies had either disappeared or were unwilling to sign on without the 10 per cent kickback that the UN was now hurriedly eliminating. See Therese Raphael, *Wall Street Journal*, 11 March 2003; Claudia Rosett, *National Review*, 10 and 21 March 2004.
[21] See for example the April 2004 Centre for Strategic and International Studies Policy Forum, 'Iraq: on the Precipice'.

the war since April 2004: 56 per cent of voters now think the invasion was a mistake. The images from Abu Ghraib have weakened the authority of the White House.

Yet those who shook their heads at the pre-emptive proclamations of the 2002 National Security Strategy have been unwilling to see it founder. With the upsurge of resistance in Iraq has come a flood of liberal imperialist advice on how to run the Occupation better. Joseph Nye laments the paucity of American TV channels capable of beaming US soft power into the Arab world. Anthony Cordesman offers recipes for more effective interrogation of prisoners. Michael Ignatieff, after deploring the painful moral juxtapositions that even sullied Reagan's funeral, warns that 'America cannot abdicate its responsibility'. Andrew Moravcsik explains: 'Europeans may find the next Iraq is a Kosovo, and they want America to intervene'.[22] Though celebrations have been muted, the UN-sponsored installation of a hireling regime in Baghdad has been all but universally hailed in the Western media as a 'positive step'.

From those who opposed the Anglo-American invasion in 2003 on the grounds that it lacked UN legitimation, or that sanctions were doing the job, there has been, understandably, a deafening silence about the future of the Occupation, broken only by murmurs about deadlines. For many, opposition to empire has been reduced to abhorrence of Bush. But the Bush administration has already implemented every step in the Democrats' programme: handover to an Iraqi government, with UN blessing and NATO involvement, as in Afghanistan. Hopes that a Kerry Administration would significantly alter current US policies in the Middle East are futile. As Clinton's foreign-policy linchpin Strobe Talbott recently explained: 'The Bush administration was right to identify Iraq as a major problem. A President Gore or McCain or Bradley would have ratcheted up the pressure, and sooner or later resorted to force'.[23] Kerry backed the invasion, will retain the Patriot Act, supports Sharon's security policies and is calling for an extra 40,000 active-duty US troops and a doubling of special forces capability. On present showing, a vote for him is little more than another bullet for Iraq. In this sense, the Bush revolution has succeeded; it has produced its heir. Whatever its colour, the next

[22] Respectively: Nye, 'America needs to use soft power', *Financial Times*, 18 April 2004; Ignatieff, *New York Times* Magazine, 27 June 2004; Moravcsik, *Financial Times*, 26 June 2004.
[23] 'The Burning of Bush', *Financial Times* magazine, 26 June 2004.

us administration will attempt to consolidate its position there. It will not be the November polls that decide the fate of the march on Baghdad. The reality is that, so long as hard blows continue to be inflicted by the resistance on the occupying army and its clients, domestic support for the recolonization of Iraq will drain away, regardless of which multi-millionaire sits in the White House.

The same holds true of Europe, where Paris and Berlin have predictably hastened to patch up their relations with Washington and approved NATO engagement to support its Baghdad regime; in the case of Chirac, sealing the pact with the Franco-American invasion of Haiti, and UN-backed overthrow of the constitutional government there. The rifts that, eighteen months ago, supposedly threatened the Atlantic alliance have been ceremoniously buried in the Normandy sands, in County Clare and Istanbul. Washington's military-imperialist thrust into Central Eurasia, at first deplored by right-minded pillars of the status quo as an over-reaching adventure, has become the basis of a new world consensus: the hegemon must not be allowed to fail. The first, elementary step against such acquiescence is solidarity with the cause of national liberation in Iraq. The us-led forces have no business there. The Iraqi *maquis* deserves full support in fighting to drive them out.

PREFACE

The presidential elections held in Taiwan this spring were widely felt within the island to be a critical moment in its history. A day before polling, incumbent candidate Chen Shui-bian, leader of the Democratic Progressive Party (DPP), was grazed by a bullet from an unknown assailant, while touring his hometown in a jeep. The ensuing sympathy gave him victory in the election by a handful of votes over his Kuomintang opponents. The mystery surrounding the shooting incident, and the tiny margin of advantage it yielded, generated heated controversy. Massive demonstrations by supporters of the Blue camp— the KMT and its allies—protested against the upshot of the poll, claiming fraud by the Green camp—the DPP and its allies. Behind this political polarization lay, among other issues, tensions between the different communities that make up Taiwan's population, about two-thirds of which is of immigrant descent from southern Fujian ('Minnan' speakers); another ten to twelve per cent of Hakka origin, mainly from Guangdong; some fifteen per cent mainlanders who arrived in the island as KMT refugees in 1949; together with a third of a million aboriginal inhabitants of the island, of Malayo-Polynesian origin.

Concerned that a divisive identity politics, playing on ethnic frictions rather than resolving them, might loom large in the electoral campaign, a distinguished group of intellectuals, artists and activists formed an Alliance for Ethnic Equality before it started. Below is an interview with four of its founders. By common consent Hou Hsiao-Hsien is one of the world's greatest film directors, whose cinema has offered a series of unforgettable portraits of Taiwanese history and society. Chu Tien-hsin is an accomplished novelist, with more than a dozen works of fiction published, of which one of the latest—The Ancient Capital— will shortly appear in English. Tang Nuo, pen-name of Hsieh Ts'ai-chün, is a leading critic and publisher, author of six volumes of essays. Hsia Chu-joe teaches architecture and planning at National Taiwan University, and has written widely on urban space and architectural theory. He has also translated Manuel Castells' trilogy The Information Age into Chinese. The interview, which covers a range of social, cultural and political issues, as well as relations between Taiwan and the mainland, was conducted a few days after the presidential election.

HOU HSIAO-HSIEN, CHU TIEN-HSIN,
TANG NUO, HSIA CHU-JOE

TENSIONS IN TAIWAN

How did the Alliance for Ethnic Equality start? What immediately inspired it?

Hou: I was not myself the initiator. Among our friends is a journalist from the *China Times* called Yang Suo. A colleague of his, Yu Fan-ying from the paper's foundation, told him that questions of ethnicity were likely to become very divisive during the election campaign, and we should get together and discuss this prospect. Many people including Tien-hsin, Tang Nuo, Chu-joe and I went there. After three or four meetings, we decided to set up the Alliance for Ethnic Equality. We wanted to warn against electoral manipulation of ethnic issues by either the Blue camp or the Green camp during the campaign. That's how the organization was set up. I was chosen to be the convenor, because I seldom say anything about political topics and am well known in Taiwan—or, as I said, I had a selling image. We started to work before the Chinese New Year, in January.

Tang: No guesswork was needed to anticipate that ethnic conflict would be whipped up again this time. It happened in each previous election, so we had a lot of experience of this. Chen Shui-bian, running for re-election as president, was at quite some disadvantage when the campaign started, and he supposedly represents the Minnan, the largest ethnic group in Taiwan. It could only benefit him if the issue of ethnicity became a major election topic, so it could be expected he would make a lot of play of it. In fact, it looked as if this might be the most serious case of identity politics ever in Taiwanese elections. That's why we set up this Alliance. Hou Hsiao-Hsien was selected because he had no political colour. In Taiwan, people tend to ask about your standpoint before you have even spoken—they want to know which side you are on. Most of the other members of the Alliance have long been involved in variously-coloured social movements; therefore they could be easily categorized as belonging to one side or another. Hou is a person without political hue. There was no vote—he was approved by acclamation.

Is it the case that democratization in Taiwan has paradoxically sharpened tensions between the different communities in the island, compared to the period of the dictatorship?

HOU: Yes. To some extent that was inevitable. In the 1970s, under the authoritarian rule of the KMT, an opposition sprang up that was already closely related to questions of ethnicity—islanders versus mainlanders—which persisted through the *Formosa* Incident.[1] But after martial law was lifted by Chiang Ching-kuo in 1987, there was a change of fronts. For two decades the opposition movement had always used the signifiers of nationalism. But after 1988, when Chiang Ching-kuo died and Lee Teng-hui succeeded him, for the first time a Taiwanese became President. That was a dramatic shift. The old mainlander forces within the KMT were increasingly marginalized by Lee, who started to cooperate with local forces, and to rely on so-called 'black channel' (*heidao*) and 'black money' (*heijin*) sources, connected to mafia and other interests. In that period, Lee and the opposition party, the DPP, were on the surface adversaries, but under the table they were supporting each other, since they both wanted to found a Taiwanese state, and based themselves on this project. So in that respect they were at one. In the election of 2000, the KMT split, allowing Chen Shui-bian to become president, to the surprise even of the DPP itself. Over the next four years, Chen's administration performed very poorly, leaving him in a weak position in the opinion polls before the election this year. So he intensified nationalist appeals, calling for the building of a nation-state in Taiwan, and labelling the Blue camp fellow-travellers of the CCP.[2]

---

[1] In August 1979, an opposition journal named *Meilidao* (Beautiful Island, ie: Formosa) appeared, publishing articles critical of the lack of social justice and democracy in Taiwan, which soon gained such popularity that it became the focus of a broad public movement. When it called for rallies to celebrate International Human Rights Day in December, the police broke up the demonstration held in Kaohsiung, and then arrested and tortured eight of its leaders, who were sentenced to long terms of imprisonment.
[2] Acronyms: KMT (Kuomintang); DPP (Democratic Progressive Party); CCP (Chinese Communist Party); PRC (People's Republic of China); ROC (Republic of China).

The DPP had been promoting 'localization' during his four years' administration, a policy affecting all areas of life, education and culture. The accumulation of measures had already generated very clear antagonisms. Many people in Taiwan felt increasingly perplexed. For instance in education, they wanted children to learn Minnan. Then there were protests—others saying that this could not simply be taken as the language of Taiwan, and questioning whether Hakka should not be taught as well. Since the government wasn't principled, it added Hakka. Then aboriginal languages were also considered. The result was to make life miserable for pupils in our elementary schools. It is the same thing in government offices, in municipalities or in Taipei. Since we have Chen as president, a chairman of a meeting may give a speech in Minnan. If anyone in the audience questions this, he will be upset. But no-one has decided to make Minnan the official language of the island yet. Such confusions now arise everywhere. For example, Minnan has suddenly appeared in the examinations for the civil service. But most applicants cannot understand it, since Taiwan has now experienced quite a lengthy period of economic growth and urbanization, producing a new social mixture in the cities. Mandarin has been taught in our schools for a long time, but now all of a sudden Minnan is required in national exams, with questions people often cannot understand, let alone answer. In this sense, so-called localization is simply Minnanization, excluding everything else. This is a programme of 'de-Sinicization', as some of its supporters term it, which continuously appears in each domain, and arouses strong repugnance. Since it got under way, we have had a more or less serious sense of being threatened.

TANG: You've asked whether there is a paradoxical relationship between democracy and ethnicity here. We should be able to avoid this in Taiwan, and in fact it's generally believed that ethnic conflicts in Taiwan are not serious among Hakka, Minnan and mainlanders, since these communities are not distinguishable in religion, dress, occupation or lifestyle. There are some genuine ethnic tensions, but these focus rather around the original inhabitants of the island, the native Taiwanese, and the new immigrants from contemporary Southeast Asia or elsewhere. But if the issue of ethnicity has nevertheless become so central in public life, this is not as a serious social phenomenon within the majority groups on the island, but rather as a product of political struggle. Most people would concede this. The KMT arrived from the mainland after the war and established a dictatorship that excluded the islanders from much political participation. Therefore when the opposition movement started, before the lifting of martial law, it wore two kinds of colours. One was localization, the colour of Taiwan. The other was that of the Left, because the KMT was a right-wing political party. But quite soon, the Left was driven out of the political arena. Between localization and the Left, the movement chose localization. When Lee Teng-hui took over as the first Taiwanese president, the opposition lost much of its *raison d'être* because an islander was already in power. From that time on, the 'ethnic' question started to change character, in a dynamic culminating in the 2004 presidential election. It was no longer an opposition between islanders and mainlanders, but between Taiwan and the CCP in Beijing. Nationalism increasingly became a convenient way of avoiding social realities, problems in the economy, education and culture. It was also, of course, the best instrument for battling against the KMT. This is the mechanism the French scholar René Girard has described in his writings on the scapegoat. When the nation faces an external crisis or threat of invasion, it is the best moment for a ruler to call for unity and to ask for a blank cheque from the people. The KMT happens to be a party originally from the mainland. Therefore, from the later period of Lee Teng-hui through to the earlier period of Chen Shui-bian's administration, ethnic manipulation in Taiwan changed from local community conflicts to the forging of a new nationalism. However, since the US and PRC have agreed there is only one China, and Taiwan is part of it, this involves a project that cannot be talked about too openly. The result is a form of nationalism that is deeply ambiguous, suspended in a strange way somewhere between calling for Taiwanese independence and operating within the existing ROC. Ethnic tensions themselves were not a particularly serious social problem, and could have been gradually reduced within Taiwan's established democratic framework. Their fanning today is a pure product of political power struggles.

If one were to make a comparison with Ireland, where the south was traditionally nationalist and the north unionist, and popular stereotypes of each community long persisted—Catholics regarding Protestants as oppressive, unimaginative and dull, Protestants viewing Catholics as lazy, slovenly, irresponsible, and so on—has there been anything like this in Taiwan? Such prejudices are capable of producing quite a lot of suspicion and tension in daily life, apart from any political manipulation of them. Has there been any analogy in the relations between Minnan, Hakka and the mainlanders who came to Taiwan at the end of the 1940s?

TANG: Taiwan differs from Ireland in the lack of any religious factor. In earlier times, Hakkas, Minnan and mainlanders typically formed separate communities, each of whose lifestyles were slightly different. There were contrasts of music, language, and the position of women in the family. For example, Hakka women tended to be very strong in character, whereas Minnan women had a much lower status. Mainlanders had once been very patriarchal, but when they were separated from their original clans, and found themselves in a new setting on the island, couples endured the suffering of exile together—the older generation having usually stayed behind on the mainland—and so relations between them became more equal. From the sixties onwards, however, Taiwan's economy grew rapidly, and as society became more and more urbanized and intermarriage increased, a point was reached where it became difficult to tell by appearance or by accent which ethnic group a person born after 1960 came from. Some of the Hakkas, where they are still concentrated in self-contained highland communities, form an exception.

You also have to remember that our situation is very different from that of Ireland, because historical hatred and bloodshed have been so much less. The killings of the local population by KMT soldiers and police after the events of February 28, 1947 were for long a deep wound in memory. But actually the 2.28 Incident was not the most enduring political repression by the KMT. That was the White Terror of the 1950s, targeting the Left. The 2.28 Incident lasted only a few days, whereas the White Terror persisted for many years, with a huge gap in the victim tolls of the two. Neither of them were truly ethnic conflicts, but state political oppression of the population as a whole. The 2.28 Incident was in a sense an accidental conflagration; whereas the White Terror was a deliberate, concerted drive by the right-wing KMT regime to destroy any opposition to it from the Left.[3] Logically, the later revolts against the KMT in Taiwan should have been mounted from a position on the Left. But economic growth increasingly reconciled workers to their lot. Rising living standards gave them hope, while rebellion carried high risks. Moreover, developments in mainland China, once the Cultural Revolution was launched,

---

[3] On February 28, 1947 a spontaneous rising by islanders against KMT misrule erupted in Taipei, which then spread to other towns. Chiang Kai-shek dispatched troops from the mainland to crush the revolt, killing somewhere between 8,000 and 20,000 people, and possibly twice that number. The White Terror began after Chiang Kai-shek had relocated to Taiwan in 1949, and continued through the 1950s, with perhaps as many as 45,000 executions.

compromised the very idea of a Left in Taiwan. The Left needed to be based on theories, while identity politics needed only to appeal to emotions. So the opposition movement in Taiwan shifted away from a Left that had been traumatized in its deep theoretical bases, to an ethnic agenda that was less fraught, which then evolved in the way we've talked about. Today it is an instrument of local power-politics. This is our major aversion. It is like a Pandora's box whose lid has been deliberately opened by politicians. The dying ethnic issue has surfaced again.

Hou: Taiwan is also not like Ireland for other reasons. Everyone shares the same religion here, but no-one strives for independence as eagerly as they've done there. Our politicians promote localization in a very crude way. They do not stick to the issue of independence and work towards it, either step by step or with a more radical approach. Their supporters only brandish rather simplistically such slogans as de-Sinicization. Actually we never believe that they can seriously carry out independence.

Hsia: Even most fundamentalists of Taiwan independence would admit that they do not plan to sacrifice their lives for this ideal. Indeed they insist it is a must to sleep soundly at home when engaged in a political movement. They say they can talk and act to maintain the movement in the daytime, but in the evening they have to go home and rest.

Hou: Much of the reason for the extent of their success lies in the resentment that the KMT dictatorship left behind. The elder generation of Minnan remember its repression and respond to the forces that once fought against it. That's understandable. But if you really pose them with the prospect of doing battle with the CCP to gain independence, not a single mother would be a taker. To be honest, nobody is willing to go to war.

If there are so few cultural distinctions between the various communities on the island today, and a great deal of intermarriage and social mixing, what explains the very marked regional pattern of the vote in Taiwanese elections? The current one is more pronounced than ever. If one looks at the election map, it's not even a patchwork—the south is Green, and the north is Blue, virtually en bloc, with scattered enclaves of the opposite camp here and there. Normally, that kind of distribution reflects either an acute social polarization or distinct cultural identities. What explains it in this case? Another question would be this: if ethnic appeals sway mostly older people who suffered under the KMT dictatorship, why has the DPP scored best among the younger generation?

CHU: Let me say something. From my own observation, I would very much confirm the belief that ethnic problems were not a big issue before. I myself am a typical example. My father came from the mainland in 1949. My mother is Hakka. So I could be labelled a 'second-generation mainlander'. But in my own experience, issues of identity—which community one belonged to—were not a significant problem until the last decade, when they started to be taken up for political ends. Since then, what was once make-believe has become reality. When Lee Teng-hui was in power, he wanted to drive those he had marginalized within the KMT out of power; these were mostly officials who had come from the mainland in 1949. For that purpose, he formed an alliance with the DPP, whose following was essentially Minnan, using the issue of ethnicity to appeal to the DPP, since he came from the same community. The main theme of his rule was that we Taiwanese should unite against mainlanders and eliminate the remaining influence of the foreign regime that descended on us from the other side of the straits. That slogan has now been declaimed for more than a decade, and has been very effective. Time and again it allowed the DPP to abandon completely its responsibilities as an opposition party in a democratic system, on the pretext that it could not risk threatening Lee Teng-hui's rule and restoring the mainlanders' power. This is our major dissatisfaction.

As for the graphic distinction between the north and the south, I take a different view of it. One often hears it said that historically the KMT valued the north above the south, because the capital was in the north, so they invested more in Taipei, while starving the agricultural counties in the south of resources. That would then explain why the north votes Blue, and the south Green. The reality, however, is that southern agricultural counties like Yunlin, Chiai and Tainan are forever faithful voters for whichever is the ruling party of the hour. They are neither Green nor Blue as such. In the election of 2000, Yunlin, Chiai and Tainan were solidly Blue—they all supported KMT, as a guaranteed bloc. This year they all voted Green. Have local beliefs changed? Not at all. They just vote for whoever is in power, in much the way that agricultural counties in Japan have almost always supported the LDP. In these areas, local people have limited access to information, and their educational level is low. In the cities, people can exchange information and ideas in many ways, via the internet, television, newspapers, magazines, or circles of friends, encouraging independence of thought. In agricultural counties, it is quite different. Most people cannot even understand Mandarin. Often their sole channel of information is the powerful ruling party, through either the official broadcasting or leaflets distributed by local government offices in the villages. Thus they always tend to vote for the party in power. If you understand this, you won't be surprised why they can all turn Green or Blue overnight. If my explanation is correct, you will not be surprised to find that the Blue vote is not only in the north but in urbanized areas generally. In the middle zones of Taiwan, such as Taichung County and Taichung City, the Blue camp did slightly less well than predicted in opinion polls this time, but they went mainly Blue in previous local elections. The reason is simply that voters are—relatively speaking—capable of more independent judgement in semi-urbanized areas.

Moreover, in a cross-section analysis of party support in various opinion polls, probably everyone, including both the DPP and the KMT themselves, would acknowledge that the KMT's major strength lies among people in their thirties and forties. Its electorate is spindle-shaped, gradually decreasing towards the two ends of old age and youth. The level of education among Blue voters is relatively high, many having college degrees. This camp also enjoys more support among women. The polls show that most of the DPP's supporters tend to be older, people in their fifties and sixties, with less education. Generally speaking, if Taiwanese society wants to move forward, it would be reasonable to think that it should not depend so much on the too young or too old, the generations that point either to a future that is still some way off, or to a past that has now already receded.

HSIA: To some extent, I agree with Tien-hsin that 'Green south and Blue north' is a political construction of the past decade, or even the last five years. It was not like this before. Working in urban studies, I incline to believe that globalization has been the principal cause of this political distribution. In competition on the world market, Taiwan's best performance comes from the high-tech corridor between Taipei and Hsinchu. Our electronics industry is the most successful sector of our economy. It also invests more than any other in the mainland. So in a global setting, the most competitive region of the country is the north. The south used to be the centre of our heavy industry. But Taiwan can no longer sustain that kind of manufacturing. In the past, the productivity of the port of Kaohsiung ranked third in the world for its handling of cargo, after Hong Kong and Singapore. It continues to enjoy many natural advantages—freighters of any size or generation can dock there, unlike Shanghai, which is having to build new ports on the Yangshan Islands.

Nevertheless, Kaohsiung has now fallen far behind not only Hong Kong and Singapore, but is losing ground to Pusan and Shanghai. Why? One reason has certainly been political, the lack of any breakthrough in relations with the mainland. But more generally, a serious regional disparity has opened up with Taipei in global capitalist competition and the transition to a post-industrial economy. Politically, however, this uneven development has been displaced into identity politics, as if the regional distinction between the north and the south were essentially a question of ethnicity. This is really troubling.

Historically, the agricultural counties in Taiwan were all Blue. They were the firmest supporters of the KMT, whereas the stronghold of opposition to Chiang Kai-shek's regime—there was no DPP yet—was Taipei. That was so from the time of Kao Yu-shu, the first Taiwanese mayor of Taipei, when you could get killed for standing up to the KMT. People in the capital have long been the most open-minded, showing least trust in official propaganda. The first time Chen Shui-bian ran for an important position, he lost in his home county Tainan, which is rural. But when he ran for mayor in Taipei, he won. The city used to be the biggest supporter of the DPP, and it is extremely embarrassing for them that it has now swung against the party. Chen Shui-bian was originally very popular here. I too voted for him. But he has squandered this support. His rule as president alienated so many people in Taipei that the city has just voted heavily Blue. The DPP now claims that this is because the city is dominated by mainlanders, which is ridiculous. Pressed to explain what proportion of the inhabitants come from across the straits, they change tack and say the Minnan are so generous in character that they are willing to support mainlanders. Such ethnic explanations make no sense at all. The reality is as Tien-hsin describes it: the average level of education in Taipei is higher, women are more independent, and the citizenry is more modern in outlook.

CHU: Part of the reason for the DPP's popularity among the younger generation may be that this age group does not yet have to face the economic realities of having to support a family.

HOU: It's also because during Chen Shui-bian's tenure as Taipei mayor, and then as president, he mobilized youth culture—there were lots of mass dancing parties and celebrations held in front of City Hall, or the Presidential Palace, with a sea of 'Chen Shui-bian Caps'. The atmosphere was carnivalesque, but also somewhat idol-worshipping. It was like a fan phenomenon. Taiwan's young people are easily attracted by that.

TANG: Previously the younger generations, including the middle cohorts in society, from twenty to fifty years old, used to be the main force supporting the DPP. The age group between thirty to fifty years old has gradually changed, mainly because of higher unemployment in recent years, and other economic problems. But the age group between twenty and thirty remains relatively unaffected. Some of the reasons have just been mentioned. They typically have no family to support and are not that concerned with economic pressures. But it also has to do with the leadership of the two political camps. Chen is much younger than either James Soong or Lien Chan, and consciously plays the card of his age.[4] Compared with them, he is naturally more attractive to young people. But when he competes with Ma Ying-jeou, the current KMT mayor in Taipei, who defeated him for the post in 1998, he does not have the same advantage. It's also true that Chen Shui-bian has put a lot of effort into wooing students and youth, including the holding of various festivities. The officials in his administration are generally quite young too. Moreover, student years are always a time of rebellion, and the DPP has reflected that spirit. It is a party that is radical in style and conduct, built on enthusiasm, that tends to break with the rules, be they moral norms or legal codes, of the establishment. It is quite an aggressive organization. The famous student movement of the early nineties, the years of the DPP's initial growth, naturally joined forces with the party. Interestingly enough, the first generation of the student movement, people now in their thirties, are among those who most frequently reject Chen Shui-bian today, because this is where unemployment is concentrated. But in the universities themselves, those remaining on campus have retained their earliest revolutionary fervour unfaded. Although the DPP competes within a democratic framework, it has always relied on something like a revolutionary dynamic in this sense. Even when it takes over power, it does not stop there, but aims at a target over the horizon, namely to found a nation—a Taiwan Republic, with its own independent constitution. So it stands for a kind of continual revolution. That too gives it a strong appeal to the younger generation, especially among university students.

---

[4] James Soong: former secretary to Chiang Ching-kuo, who was the KMT's provincial governor of the island in the nineties, and now heads the People First Party, for which he ran as vice-presidential candidate on the Blue ticket in 2004. Lien Chan: former KMT premier under Lee Teng-hui in the nineties, and the party's presidential candidate in 2004.

Why do the Hakka communities in Taiwan vote solidly Blue?

TANG: They don't—rather, they vote solidly against Chen.

CHU: Exactly: it's the other way around. They refuse to vote Green.

HOU: Their situation is like this. I'm a Hakka myself, but I was brought to Taiwan by my family in 1947 right after I was born. Basically I am what they call 'mainland Hakka'. When I was a boy, I refused to admit this because my schoolmates all said that Hakkas were mean and stingy. Such stereotypes were very strong. Therefore I absolutely would not admit that I was a Hakka in my childhood. Later, I found that Hakkas tended to live in highland areas of agricultural counties, in self-contained groups with a very strong sense of clan self-protection. They were conservative in their ways, and had long been on bad terms with the much more numerous Minnan. Since they had so often been attacked or threatened in the past, going right back to the seventeenth century, Hakkas were reluctant to marry Minnan, or into any other ethnic group. Their rate of inter-marriage was always low. So after the KMT arrived from the mainland, maybe they looked to the Blue camp as some sort of shield.

CHU: Let me add something. Because my mother is Hakka, most of my relatives are Hakkas. I believe we should say that they have received neither preferential treatment nor special humiliation or oppression from the KMT, so their attitude towards the KMT is to stay at a respectful distance from it. But they are scared by Minnan and dislike them very much, because historically there were so many violent conflicts fought between these two ethnic groups. We have a saying that Zhangzhou people and Quanzhou people came to Taiwan one after another. Then there were Minnan and Hakka. Many died in the fights between them. So they have been enemies for ages. Tang Nuo is right to point out that Hakkas fear the Green rather than trust the Blue. The Green's ethnic base is the Minnan population who make up about 70 per cent of Taiwan's total population, and they have shown some increasingly exclusivist tendencies in recent years. They talk continuously about the Taiwanese people or the Taiwanese language, but these usages do not include the Hakka. They are referring only to the Minnan. That's why some Hakkas would reply, 'the state you want to establish is yours—we didn't say we wanted to found a state: have you ever listened to us? If in your Republic of Taiwan, it is only the Minnan who are going to rule and become masters of the country, then what's the difference from the mainlanders ruling us, as it used to be? We are still the same, the ruled. Therefore we are not at all interested in your nation-building project.' I think this is their basic attitude.

You have all been talking about the DPP's manipulation of identity politics. But if someone says to you—yes, we must do everything to fight the stoking-up of ethnic tensions in Taiwan, but we should also try to move ahead together towards an independent Tawianese state, in which there is ethnic equality, would you agree to that?

HOU: Yes, we certainly agree.

TANG: No, we will be extremely alarmed.

CHU: Exactly.

HSIA: Isn't this hypothetical?

TANG: We have historical lessons in this respect. Our experience in Taiwan is that when the ruling party—whichever one—starts to raise this issue, it usually wants to shift people's attention from more urgent substantial problems. Personally, I am Minnan and I don't reject the idea that Taiwan should be able to exercise various options. But I have always been sensitive to the sound of official nationalism. When you hear that voice, it is usually telling you how much you need to sacrifice for the nation. We are alert to this. In recent years, the voice of independence has become quite loud. But the essential character of Taiwan is, after all, that it is an immigrant society. It has been unwilling to face the real problem of independence seriously, namely its price. For everyone knows, that if the two sides of the Taiwan Strait were to go to war, it would be extremely high. On the whole, people here have tended to avoid thinking about this question. But if it were really posed, I don't know whether Taiwanese society, with its strong immigrant character, would still insist on independence. Nationalism should be handled extremely carefully in Taiwan, because it faces an inevitable opponent, which is the nationalism of 1.2 billion people a short distance away. I am highly skeptical whether Taiwan should move in such a dangerous direction.

CHU: I think one should adapt a slogan of the CCP's to the DPP: listen to what they say, and watch what they do. Take this election as an example. One day before the vote, the DPP told the country, over and over again, from Chen's speech to the last campaign leaflet, that if you didn't vote for them but for the Blues, you would be a fellow-traveller of mainland Communism, and effectively belong to another country. Yet after making this kind of claim, the next day people would be advised to go back to their normal life. I cannot be convinced by this. So I've spent a long time watching whether you mean what you say. Whose nation is it you are talking about? This is very important. I don't care whether it calls itself the Republic of Taiwan, or whatever. I want to know whose country it is. If it's going to be a country defined by a certain person or a certain ethnic group alone, with no space for me, then no matter what it is called, I cannot accept it. I can give you a very small example. Yesterday, I ran into a student who is studying my work in the Taiwanese department of Cheng Kung University. When she told her supervisor this, he upbraided her until she wept, telling her she should change her research topic. I asked her why. She said: 'he told me, how could you study a second-generation mainlander writer?' I asked her who her supervisor was. It turns out he was Lin Rui-ming, who is not just a professor in Cheng Kung University, but the director of the National Literary Museum, which is the highest independent unit in the field outside the Ministry of Culture, working with all writers, collecting relics or holding events. This is an official figure, who can tell his student straightforwardly not to study my work because I am a so-called second-generation mainlander. How could this kind of Taiwan Republic be meaningful to me?

HOU: When I answered your question, I said 'Yes'. What did I mean? I wasn't thinking of the current situation, but imagining the position Taiwan might occupy, if it overcame its internal problems, in the Chinese-speaking communities around the world. Also: what kind of role would it want to play in Asia? These two questions are, in my view, the most important for Taiwan's future direction. At the moment, I agree with Tang Nuo and Tien-hsin that we face a problem of mentality—an incomprehensible narrow-mindedness of the sort Tien-hsin has just described. But if we try to imagine a better future, I would say that if a Taiwanese government could truly resolve all ethnic questions, reconciling Fujianese, Hakka, mainlander, aboriginal Taiwanese and the new immigrants, through real equality and inter-marriage, then it would no doubt be capable of handling the question of Taiwan's position in the Chinese-speaking world and Taiwan's role in Asia. Of course, such a notion remains an ideal. In present conditions, we are very far from that.

Hsia: I am on the Left, but I wouldn't emphasize this issue. For a long time, one of the principles distinguishing Left and Right has been their attitude to the nation-state. The Right typically aims at founding one, while the Left has rarely put its energy into that. How and why a national identity is constructed are issues worth serious attention. They are not to be casually dismissed. In Taiwan, we need sympathetic analysis of the historical and political causes of the emergence of its modern nationalism. But we also need to remember how often, in the history of developing countries, building a nation-state has come to a bad end. If there were no more ethnic conflicts inside Taiwan, what I would look forward to is a tomorrow in which we can go beyond the idea of nation-state, towards a cross-border world. I know that we still need a state to regulate, to protect, to construct. But does it have be based on a nation? I would rather like to imagine a closer relation among Chinese-speaking cities, a kind of intercity networking in East Asia. I'd prefer to explore such new institutional possibilities. After all, they are trying to invent a new system in Europe. They didn't want to reproduce a nation-state, so now they have a European Union, which is not a super-state like the us, where there is a federal structure but basically the country is just a mega-nation-state. If we really want to think about the future, I'd rather we imagined one along these lines, instead of following a brilliant leader to create a new nation. I know it is difficult, but the price of trying to create another nation-state here would be too high—half the population would not approve it. How should we deal with a society traumatized by such a deep division?

Chu: There could be a civil war.

Tang: We more or less regard ourselves as intellectuals. The role of an intellectual is to oppose governments and criticize authority. As for the nation or the state, I often think of Graham Greene's words in *Our Man in Havana*: 'I wouldn't kill for my country. I wouldn't kill for capitalism or Communism or social democracy or the welfare state—whose welfare? I would kill Carter because he killed Hasselbacher . . . If I love or if I hate, let me love or hate as an individual. I will not be 59200/5 in anyone's global war.' So 'country' has no appeal for me. We need a wider horizon and a more universal idea than the empty concept of a nation, or something that is more substantial and closer to our sensibilities and our lives as actual individuals than anything that some latter-day version of Rousseau's civil religion could offer.

How would you describe the general situation of the arts in Taiwan today? In the mainland, cultural activities are subject to censorship by officialdom. Clearly nothing like this exists in Taiwan. Would it be right to think that the different arts can flourish here without any political controls or inspections?

TANG: No, that would be misleading. There is no censorship as such, but recent years have seen an unofficial tendency towards a kind of selection, driven by the politically correct slogans of localization and de-Sinicization. This has become a very serious pressure, especially in academic and literary life, where it is now more acute than official censorship might be. In Taiwan's universities, dissertations, funds and promotions are all controlled by the ruling party. A recent survey reported that some 80–90 per cent of doctoral and master's theses in the humanities and social sciences now concentrate on the study of Taiwan. The result is that the atmosphere has become quite tense in academic institutions, more so than in society at large. The DPP has now been in power for four years, and has put a lot of effort into bringing this area of life under its influence. Relatively speaking, the KMT was more tolerant towards culture, not because it had advanced ideas, but because it was incapable of recognizing cultural issues—it had no understanding of culture whatsoever, and no policy towards it. In such circumstances, there was actually more space for scholars and artists. The DPP, on the other hand, had very definite ideas about culture from the beginning, related to its particular attachment to the myths of nation-building, and so has been much more inclined to interfere, as if intellectual and artistic life were a battlefield. This attitude is not unique to Taiwan, of course. Nationalism is a variant of Rousseau's civil religion. As a religion, it does not encourage you to think. It only asks you to believe. It is essentially the opposite of the principle of literature and the arts.

What about the cinema?

HOU: The situation is miserable. It's not a question of censorship. Mainland films are not banned in Taiwan, but people don't go to see them. They don't even see Taiwanese films. Nowadays they only watch Hollywood movies. Taiwan produces just a dozen or so films each year, and most of them depend on official funding. There are perhaps only three exceptions—Yang Te-chang [Edward Yang], Tsaï Ming-liang and myself—who can get financing in France or Japan.[5] So the problem is one of resources. In recent years, official funding has been controlled by a group of people, whose banner is localization. These people are very narrow-minded. They lack any talent or cinematic ability themselves, but want to impose a kind of political correctness, and look for directors to make films that will illustrate it. But they don't know how to find them. So they've only made a few soap operas, on which they've spent a lot of money. But they are very concerned to exercise control, and if they can't shape software—the script or *mise en scène* of a film—they try to make up for it with hardware, by supplying or denying financial support for post-production. Control of resources matters there. I've never had any problems myself, since I'm not dependent on this circuit. The only time I encountered any problem was when I made *Flowers of Shanghai*, and I was reproached for shooting a film with a mainland setting.[6] The government has no competence in cultural questions. The official unit in charge of the film industry is hopeless. No matter how often you talk to them, they pay no attention.

In literature, their people are similarly incompetent, unable to compete with real writers. But the government takes care to put various awards and prizes under its control. Real creative artists do not care about these at all. But there are constant examples of official meddling in the arts. When there is a project in the national theatre and a performing troop has to be found, they tend to look for obedient people to stage the play, and the outcome is usually poor. People seldom go to see these productions. Another recent example is the way a list of writers invited to France was altered by the government. The DPP eliminated authors it didn't like and added authors it approved of. Tien-hsin's sister, Chu Tien-wen, was crossed off the list.[7] The French were infuriated. They said, we don't want the names you've supplied, we want those whom we invited. Eventually, the government had to back down and Tien-wen was allowed to go. That was for China's cultural year in France.

[5] See 'The Frustrated Architect' and 'Taiwan Stories', NLR 11, Sept–Oct 2001.
[6] *Flowers of Shanghai* (1998): based on an 1894 novel by Han Bangqing, set in a traditional bordello of the city in the late nineteenth century.
[7] Chu Tien-wen: well-known Taiwanese writer and collaborator with Hou, author of the script for *A City of Sadness* and other films.

HSIA: I am the convenor of the architectural group for this year's National Arts Awards, which is a new category that will start giving awards in 2004. There will also be new awards for the cinema. It is generally acknowledged that Taiwanese cinema has much greater achievements to its credit than our architecture. We have already decided, in fact, to leave this year's award blank. So far there isn't any good architecture in Taiwan. We need to make further efforts.

CHU: Today, if you apply for a position in the Chinese department of a university when someone has died or retired or taken sick leave, they will tell you the post is not being renewed. No more faculties are being added or even replaced. But if you apply for a job in departments of Taiwanese studies, Taiwanese language or Taiwanese literature, things are different. Traditionally, to set up an institute or department in Taiwan, there are certain threshold requirements, concerning syllabuses, teachers, funds and so forth. But now, if you want to establish a Taiwanese institute or department, you get immediate approval once you submit your budget. The atmosphere is such, some teachers in Chinese departments are saying that after another couple of years maybe we will be shunted into the foreign language department. The situation is similar in the schools, where pupils are under a lot of examination pressure, as in other East Asian countries, and their scores can now depend on giving the politically correct answers to questions like: what country do you belong to? I know this from my own daughter, who likes Chinese literature and told me she would rather give up high marks than be forced to say what is expected of her. But there wouldn't be many children like her. For good scores, you have to be Taiwanese. So in your school days, you internalize those ideas in your formative years.

You've spoken of the dangers of a divisive 'Taiwanization'—in effect, Minnanization—of education, culture and the civil service. But wouldn't Green supporters say: 'This is just correcting the many years of discrimination against Minnan by the KMT regime, when Mandarin was forcibly imposed on us. We are being more tolerant to Mandarin speakers than they ever were to us.' What's your view of this sort of argument, and more generally of the language and educational policies of the KMT when it was in power?

TANG: This is the worst excuse of the DPP and could become an obstacle to further social progress in Taiwan in the future. What do I mean by this? To be progressive is continuously to upgrade our criteria of performance; it is to feel that what could once be done has now become unacceptable. We often say that politics has always been the weakest link in the chain of Taiwanese development, where progress has tended to break down. For a long time, we've seen a race between society and politics in Taiwan. When society took the lead, it could improve everything else, including even politics, as happened in the period around the lifting of martial law in the late eighties. When politics took the lead, social development would be dragged backward, as has happened over the issue of ethnic tensions.

Viewed from this perspective, the DPP is in some ways more worrisome than the KMT. For the corruption of the KMT was relatively confined within the 'political' sphere in a more restricted sense. The party did not concern itself overmuch with the economic, cultural or educational spheres. The DPP, however, wants to meddle in all these realms to serve its political ends. For example, it handles the issue of cross-straits trade from a single-mindedly party-political position. Similarly, it has raided or sued newspaper offices, bought up news media firms with public funds or money from private conglomerates, injected its political ideology into educational reform and textbook revision and so forth. The KMT committed similar mistakes before, but on a lesser scale and without the same extent of social damage. Since the DPP came to power, many people have become anxious—not just about their economic situation, but about the withering away of social life in general. Politics is getting the upper hand over the whole society. More than any particular phenomena, it is this trend that is the gravest cause for concern today.

CHU: When the DPP says: 'if the KMT could do this before, why couldn't we do the same now?', it reminds us that to observe a political party, it is not enough to look at its performance in opposition, we must also see how it uses its power after coming to office. If we do that, we can only conclude that the DPP is in practice not that different from the KMT. This ought to be a disappointment to many intellectuals and ordinary citizens who have long supported the DPP and had high expectations of it. Yet I believe this may not be an unhealthy way to view the situation. Both Blue and Green camps then lose their mystic haloes, and therewith certain burdens as well; they fall back to the earth of normal competition between parties in a constitutional democracy, in which neither is any more sacred nor more evil than the other. Seen in that light, this is not a bad development at all.

Hou: Taiwan has a folk saying: 'As soon as you get over a cough, you get asthma'. If the DPP is itself willing to be asthmatic, that is its own degeneration. Or to put it more crudely, if other people are dung beetles, and you want to be such beetles too, what choice is there for us but to get rid of you?

Hsia: We shouldn't reproduce the discrimination and ideology of the KMT regime. We need change, to change ourselves—this is the social transformation we expect. Otherwise, we would just reproduce the same logic as before. Isn't that the lesson of Lao She's *Tea House*?[8]

How do you envisage the future activities of the Alliance?

Tang: Before the presidential election, we had just one aim: to prevent further fanning of ethnic tensions during the campaign. Our original intention was that, if either of the two sides, Blue or Green, manipulated issues of ethnicity, we would stand up and stop them. With that immediate urgency prior to the election, when the whole society was charged with high tension, it was not easy to talk about long-term plans or theoretical constructions. Now that the election is over, we can develop a set of projects more gradually. We have some immediate plans to promote legislation against ethnic discrimination—in other words, a bill of equal rights. We will also press for commissions to be set up to establish the historical truth about our past, including the February 28 Incident and the White Terror, so that people don't have just to guess what happened, as they do now. We want to see the archives properly opened to the public, under professional guidelines set by the historical profession and by law. We incorporated this demand in our inaugural manifesto. Another issue that we insist needs to be faced is the situation of new immigrants in Taiwan today. Many of these are 'brides' from the mainland, or from Malaysia, Indonesia and Vietnam. They usually live in the countryside in Taiwan. The babies of these brides now account for one out of eight of Taiwan's newborn population. If discrimination against them persists, this will very soon become a big social problem. There are also, of course, the long-standing difficulties suffered by the aboriginal peoples of our island.

---

[8] Three-act play (1957) by Lao She, set in Qing, Republican and immediate post-war China, in which the same repressive roles are reproduced from one period and generation to the next.

Our initial intention was to extract some promises of restraint from the two camps while our voice could still be heard during the election. Many of us had been active in various particular fields—cultural activities or social movements. Some were engaged in working with aboriginal Taiwanese, others with foreign labourers and immigrants; still others in women's movements. This time we came together because of the nature of the Alliance. Though we have had limited success so far, the experience has been very positive, since we have realized that when we are united we become more imaginative and more effective.

CHU: I would put it this way. Whereas social movements primarily face towards the people, or the public, the Alliance faces towards power-holders and political parties. Social movements agitate and educate. Our role will to be check and criticize. That doesn't mean we don't care about people. Actually we are all active in our own fields, working towards people's positions. For example, Hou Hsiao-Hsien faces his audience, Tang Nuo and I towards our readers, Hsia his students, and social activists their public. I believe the job of the Alliance is to face the authorities, and speak with a critical voice to them.

HOU: Each of our members has long been active in their own field. In the cinema, aside from making my own films, I've also set up an association to organize different events. When I became more familiar with fellow members of the Alliance, I noticed that some of them had been working to help those with work-related injuries, others with aboriginals, others with foreign labourers. Their cases—like such historical events in Taiwan as the February 28 Incident and the White Terror, about which as producer I made two documentaries—reminded me that filmmakers could provide certain resources to collaborate with them. For example, we can make television documentaries, an hour or an hour and a half each time. These activists have a rich experience in their own areas of work, but the social movements they represent have a very hard time becoming visible in the media. It is extremely difficult for them to reach the public. The media do not care about them at all. So if we can make visual images of what they are doing, we may be able to empower them. We've discussed this, and will organize a team to work on such projects. In that sense, as well as criticizing the authorities, our Alliance also wants to do something to increase communication between different ethnic and disadvantaged groups, to help them understand each other better, so we can see what the opportunities are for change. Even if they seem dim, we still need to try.

TANG: We also have to be able to speak honestly about nationalism. Taiwan has little experience of the scale of disaster that ethnic conflicts can bring. In principle, as a late-developing society, Taiwan could draw on the experience of Europe, of Central Asia and Southeast Asia. But there are two ways of learning. One is by acquiring historical knowledge, so that we can turn other people's experience to our own benefit, and not pay so high a price for it. The other is to learn by one's own suffering. Europe had to endure two world wars before it understood that there are things human beings should never do to each other. In Taiwan, we don't know which of these two ways of learning will prevail. We don't know if we can convince our next generation by using examples and words. We don't know if only disaster and pain can awaken them. There is currently a race in Taiwan between these possibilities: learning by knowledge or by calamity. We hope we can convince people, so that the society does not have to pay that price. But frankly, we don't have any assurance at all. For today's Taiwan is very indifferent towards other people's experience. Besides, when any nationalism emerges, it usually defines itself as unlike anything else—other people's experience is not the same as ours, we have our own national conditions, and our own unique path. Other experiences are irrelevant. But if we look around us, we can see that Taiwan is not that unique. Much that has happened and is still happening here was lived through by others elsewhere. This is why we are so worried about the rise of an anti-intellectual, populist nationalism in this island, and have a duty to warn of the dangers it ignores, in rejecting so much of the real experience of human history and the opportunity to avoid repeating its disasters.

This is a question for Hou Hsiao-Hsien. You are world-famous as the director of a trilogy of films about the history of Taiwan: The Puppet Master on the era of Japanese colonial rule; A City of Sadness on the February 28 Incident; Good Men, Good Women on the period of the White Terror. Do you have any plans to make films on later periods of your history, episodes or themes after the 1950s?

HOU: I think that should be done by younger generations. The trilogy of films I made was closer to the background of my own age-group. They were concerned with experiences that shaped the lives of the generations just before mine. It was like shooting part of my own experience. I always wonder, why don't the directors who are ten or twenty years younger than I am record what was happening just before they grew up? We cannot record those experiences for them. The story of the opposition movement against the KMT dictatorship, the *Formosa* Incident—all that should be re-imagined by their generation rather than mine. Personally, after the films I made on Japanese occupation, the February 28 Incident, and the White Terror, which were based on what we heard from the elder generation and could learn from literature, I don't feel the strength to repeat this. Perhaps it is a matter of distance in time. I have moved to another stage in my own creative work, and it's difficult to go back to an earlier one. But I think some of those themes remain highly suitable for television films. My films on those topics were by no means comprehensive. There are lots of historical episodes and figures missing from them. Chen Ying-chen of the Jen Chian (Human Realm) Study Society, is trying to use images and films to present some of this history, and I've had discussions with them. There are lots of themes to work on. I will probably supervise and produce some films for them—organize a team, or let them organize a team, for this purpose. They've already started. They came to me for help, to provide equipment and negatives, because I have more resources. I've started to assist them.

Edward Yang told us a couple of years ago that he thought it would be impossible for him to make a film about ethnic tensions, for example between Fujianese and former mainlanders, in Taiwan. Would you also say that such contemporary social realities can't be represented on the screen today?

Hou: No, I think it's possible to make a film of this kind. The important thing would be to have enough cultural preparation, to have the right sense of the subject. I am now starting to make films entirely focussed on contemporary themes. Since *Flowers of Shanghai*, I have been returning to modern times, and thinking about the difficulties of representing them. Films cannot treat these as exhaustively as television or newspaper reports. So I have been wrestling with the problem of what angles or forms to adopt for them in the cinema. I don't think my ideas are very finely tuned yet, but I do feel that political issues always penetrate into daily life, and that to present that life from within would be the best way of tackling the issues you mention. Now that I have joined the Alliance, I might get some ideas from it that would move me in that direction. It is hard to say.

A final question about your current movies. There is one clear continuity between your earlier films and your latest ones, which is your interest in the situation of young people. But how would you describe the differences between the worlds conjured up in The Boys from Feng kuei *(1982) and in* Millennium Mambo *(2002)? Obviously, there are spatial and temporal distances—the former is about youngsters from the offshore islands when Taiwan was still a predominantly small-town and rural society, while the latter depicts metropolitan life in the new century. But what are the existential contrasts in these two epochs and settings for young people themselves, in your eyes?*

HOU: Let me answer that by saying something about my new film *Coffee Time*, which was shot in Japan. In one sense, it is a purely Japanese story, which I made in homage to Yasujiro Ozu on the centenary of his birth. Ozu made films on family themes, for example the predicaments of a father in marrying off a daughter. In Tokyo today, these daughters have now entered into a new state of being, identical to that of many of their contemporaries in Taiwan. So I adapted phenomena in Taiwan with which I'm familiar. We have many single mothers, about 300,000 according to official statistics. Typically, such a young mother is about thirty. She becomes pregnant accidentally with a boyfriend. She decides to have the child, but does not tell her partner. She is not going to marry him either. She wants to bring the baby up all by herself. She thinks that love is too tiring, relations between men and women have become too exhausting. Besides, she has learnt from her own family experience that she could be more devoted to her child if she doesn't have to waste time solving conflicts with a husband. I borrowed this phenomenon from Taiwan and filmed it in Japan. In the movie, the girl's boyfriend is Taiwanese. I based him on the experience of a schoolmate of my own daughter. She went to university in the US, where many of her classmates came from families that ran small or middle-sized firms in Taiwan and then emigrated to Thailand, because production costs were lower there. So their children had their elementary and secondary education in Thailand. Then they went to university in the US, studying subjects related to their family business. For example, if the family made tyres or leather, the child would study chemistry; if the family made umbrellas, the child would study management. Anyway, they studied whatever their parents wanted them to. They have all graduated now, and they are all working in their father's family factory. Nowadays those factories have moved from Thailand to mainland China, or Hong Kong. My daughter had many such schoolmates.

This interested me very much. So I combined this background with Taiwan's single mother pattern in my film and moved the story to Japan. Perhaps in the future young people will not be so fixed in a given place as they used to be. They may have some experience of mainland China, of Hong Kong, or of other cities in Asia. Or they may have studied in the US or Europe. This is very common in Taiwan. Often their experience of other countries is far more than that of the island itself. Their time in Taiwan may be quite limited. Many of my daughter's schoolmates went abroad while in middle school, and the earlier they go abroad, the harder it is for them to come back to Taiwan, because they are not used to its ways. Those who go abroad after graduating from high school are more acclimatized to Taiwan; those who leave after university still more so. There are now also many young Taiwanese who go to universities in the mainland. For example, the son of one of my schoolmates who is also a film director, Hsu Hsiao-ming, went to Beijing after studying at the National Taiwan University for one year. He didn't like the experience and insisted on studying in Beijing. Nowadays, young people share information, as well as much the same experience and memories, everywhere. Regional differences have faded. They listen to the same music. For them, unlike our generation, everything is similar. Their world has changed. I always say, why can't the DPP leave the possibility of nation-building, or many other options, to our next generation? How do you know what they are capable of? You should just mind your own business and leave resources to them. Perhaps their way of handling things will be far simpler than you imagine.

Taipei, 23 March 2004

FRANCO MORETTI

GRAPHS, MAPS, TREES

Abstract Models for Literary History—3

REES; EVOLUTIONARY THEORY. They come last, in this series of essays, but were really the beginning, as my Marxist formation, influenced by DellaVolpe and his school, entailed a great respect (in principle, at least) for the methods of the natural sciences.[1] So, at some point I began to study evolutionary theory, and eventually realized that it opened a unique perspective on that key issue of literary study which is the interplay between history and form. Theories of form are usually blind to history, and historical work blind to form; but in evolution, morphology and history are really the two sides of the same coin. Or perhaps, one should say, they are the two dimensions of the same tree.

I

Figure 1 (overleaf) reproduces the only tree—'an odd looking affair, but indispensable', as Darwin writes to his publisher in the spring of 1859[2]—in *The Origin of Species*; it appears in the fourth chapter, 'Natural selection' (which in later editions becomes 'Natural selection; or, the survival of the fittest'), in the section on 'Divergence of character'. But when the image is first introduced, Darwin does not call it a 'tree':[3]

> Now let us see how this principle of great benefit being derived from divergence of character, combined with the principles of natural selection and of extinction, will tend to act. The accompanying diagram will aid us in understanding this rather perplexing subject . . .[4]

FIGURE 1: *Divergence of character*

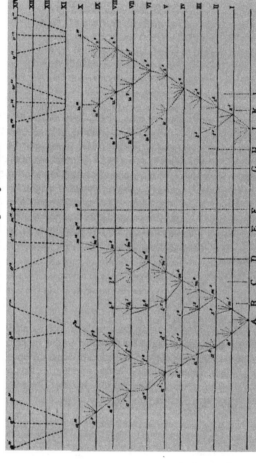

Let A be a common, widely-diffused, and varying species, belonging to a genus large in its own country. The little fan of diverging dotted lines of unequal lengths proceeding from A may represent its varying offspring.... Only those variations which are in some way profitable will be preserved or naturally selected. And here the importance of the principle of benefit being derived from divergence of character comes in; for this will generally lead to the most different or divergent variations (represented by the outer dotted lines) being preserved and accumulated by natural selection.

Charles Darwin, *On the Origin of Species*

A diagram. After the diachronic diagrams of the first article, and the spatial ones of the second, trees are a way of constructing *morphological* diagrams, with form and history as the two variables of the analysis: the vertical axis of figure 1 charting the regular passage of time (every interval, writes Darwin, 'one thousand generations'), and the horizontal axis following the formal diversification ('the little fans of diverging dotted lines') that would eventually lead to 'well-marked varieties', or to entirely new species.

The horizontal axis follows formal diversification . . . But Darwin's words are stronger: he speaks of 'this rather perplexing subject'—elsewhere, 'perplexing & unintelligible'—whereby forms don't just 'change', but change by always *diverging* from each other (remember, we are in the section on 'Divergence of Character').[6] Whether as a result of historical

---

[1] The first two essays in this series, on 'Graphs' and 'Maps', appeared respectively in NLR 24, November–December 2003 and NLR 26, March–April 2004.

[2] 'It is an odd looking affair, but is *indispensable*', continues the letter to John Murray of May 31, 1859, 'to show the nature of the very complex affinities of past & present animals'. Frederick Burkhardt and Sydney Smith, eds, *The Correspondence of Charles Darwin*, vol. VII (1858–59), Cambridge 1991, p. 300.

[3] The word 'tree' appears only at the end of the chapter, and surrounded by signs of hesitation, possibly because of the religious echoes associated with the Tree of Life: 'The affinities of all the beings of the same class have *sometimes* been represented by a great tree. I *believe* this simile *largely* speaks the truth': Charles Darwin, *The Origin of Species*, 1859; facsimile of the first edition, Cambridge, MA 2001, p. 129 (italics mine).

[4] Darwin, *Origin*, p. 116.

[5] 'You will find Ch. IV perplexing & unintelligible', he writes to Lyell on September 2, 1859, 'without the aid of enclosed queer Diagram, of which I send old & useless proof': Burkhardt and Smith, eds, *Correspondence of Charles Darwin*, p. 329.

[6] 'The intent of Darwin's famous diagram has almost always been misunderstood', writes Stephen Jay Gould: 'Darwin did not draw this unique diagram simply to illustrate the generality of evolutionary branching, but primarily to explicate the principle of divergence. Darwin's solution . . . holds that natural selection will generally favor the most extreme, the most different, the most divergent forms in a spectrum of variation emanating from any common parental stock. . . . Note how only two species of the original array (A–L) ultimately leave descendants—the left extreme A and the near right extreme I. Note how each diversifying species first generates an upward fan of variants about its modal form, and how only the peripheral populations of the fan survive to diversify further. Note that the total morphospace (horizontal axis) expands by divergence, although only two of the original species leave descendants.' Stephen Jay Gould, *The Structure of Evolutionary Theory*, Cambridge, MA 2002, pp. 228–9, 235–6.

accidents, then, or under the action of a specific 'principle',[7] the reality of divergence pervades the history of life, defining its morphospace—its space-of-forms: an important concept, in the pages that follow—as an intrinsically expanding one.

From a single common origin, to an immense variety of solutions: it is this incessant growing-apart of life forms that the branches of a morphological tree capture with such intuitive force. 'A tree can be viewed *as a simplified description of a matrix of distances*', write Cavalli-Sforza, Menozzi and Piazza in the methodological prelude to their *History and Geography of Human Genes*; and figure 2, with its mirror-like alignment of genetic groups and linguistic families drifting away from each other (in a 'correspondence [that] is remarkably high but not perfect', as they note with aristocratic aplomb),[8] makes clear what they mean: a tree is a way of sketching *how far* a certain language has moved from another one, or from their common point of origin.

And if language evolves by diverging, why not literature too?

II

For Darwin, 'divergence of character' interacts throughout history with 'natural selection and extinction': as variations grow apart from each other, selection intervenes, allowing only a few to survive. In a seminar of a few years ago, I addressed the analogous problem of literary survival, using as a test case the early stages of British detective fiction. We chose clues as the trait whose transformations were likely to be most revealing for the history of the genre, and proceeded to chart the relationships

---

[7] 'One might say . . . that 'divergence of character' requires no separate principle beyond adaptation, natural selection, and historical contingency . . . Climates alter; topography changes; populations become isolated, and some, adapting to modified environments, form new species. What more do we need? . . . But Darwin grew dissatisfied with a theory that featured a general principle to explain adaptation, but then relied upon historical accidents of changing environments to resolve diversity. He decided that a fully adequate theory of evolution required an equally strong principle of diversity, one that acted intrinsically and predictably': Gould, *Structure*, p. 226.

[8] Luigi Luca Cavalli-Sforza, Paolo Menozzi and Alberto Piazza, *The History and Geography of Human Genes*, Princeton 1994, pp. 38, 99 (italics mine).

1710 and 1850, for instance (figure 2 of 'Graphs'), *Pride and Prejudice* and *The life of Pill Garlick; rather a whimsical sort of fellow*, appear as exactly alike: two dots in the 1813 column, impossible to tell apart. But figures 3 and 4 aim precisely at *distinguishing* 'The Red-Headed League' from 'The Assyrian Rejuvenator' and 'How He Cut His Stick', thus establishing an intelligible relationship between canonical and non-canonical branches.

IV

Trees; or, divergence in literary history. But this view of culture usually encounters a very explicit objection. 'Among the many differences in deep principle between natural evolution and cultural change', writes Stephen Jay Gould, their 'topology'—that is to say, the abstract overall shape of natural and cultural history—is easily the most significant:

> Darwinian evolution at the species level and above is a story of continuous and irreversible proliferation . . . a process of constant separation and distinction. Cultural change, on the other hand, receives a powerful boost from amalgamation and anastomosis of different traditions. A clever traveller may take one look at a foreign wheel, import the invention back home, and change his local culture fundamentally and forever.[11]

The traveller and his wheel are not a great example (they are a case of simple diffusion, not of amalgamation), but the general point is clear, and is frequently made by historians of technology. George Basalla:

> Different biological species usually do not interbreed, and on the rare occasions when they do their offspring are infertile. Artifactual types, on the other hand, are routinely combined to produce new and fruitful entities . . . The internal combustion engine branch was joined with that of the bicycle and horse-drawn carriage to create the automobile branch, which in turn merged with the dray wagon to produce the motor truck.[12]

Artifactual species combined in new and fruitful entities: in support of his thesis, Basalla reproduces Alfred Kroeber's ingenious 'tree of culture' (figure 5, overleaf), whose Alice-in-Wonderland quality makes the reality of convergence unforgettably clear. As it should be, because convergence is indeed a major factor of cultural evolution. But is it *the only one?*

[11] Stephen Jay Gould, *Full House. The Spread of Excellence from Plato to Darwin*, New York 1996, pp. 220–1
[12] George Basalla, *The Evolution of Technology*, Cambridge 1988, pp. 137–8.

FIGURE 5: *Tree of Culture*

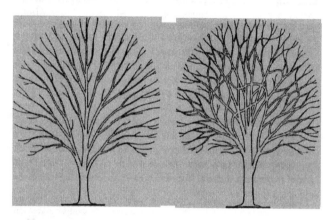

THE TREE OF LIFE AND THE TREE OF THE KNOWLEDGE OF
GOOD AND EVIL—THAT IS, OF HUMAN CULTURE

The course of organic evolution can be portrayed properly as a tree of life, as Darwin
has called it, with trunk, limbs, branches, and twigs. The course of development of
human culture in history cannot be so described, even metaphorically. There is a constant
branching-out, but the branches also grow together again, wholly or partially, all the
time. Culture diverges, but it syncretizes and anastomoses too. Life really does nothing
but diverge: its occasional convergences are superficial resemblances, not a joining or a
reabsorption. A branch on the tree of life may approach another branch; it will not normally
coalesce with it. The tree of culture, on the contrary, is a ramification of such coalescences,
assimilations, or acculturations. This schematic diagram visualizes this contrast.

Alfred Kroeber, *Anthropology*

'*Culture diverges*, but it syncretizes and anastomoses too', runs Kroeber's
comment to the tree of culture; and Basalla: 'the oldest surviving made
things . . . stand at the beginning of the *interconnected, branching*, continu-
ous series of artifacts shaped by deliberate human effort'. Interconnected
and branching; syncretism *and* divergence: rather than irreconcilable
'differences in deep principle' between convergence and divergence,
passages like these (which could be easily multiplied) suggest a sort of

division of labour between them; or perhaps, better, a cycle to which they both contribute in turn. Convergence, I mean, only arises *on the basis of previous divergence*, and the power of its results tends in fact to be directly proportional to the distance between the original branches (bicycles, and internal combustion engines). Conversely, a successful convergence usually produces *a powerful new burst of divergence*: like the 'new evolutionary series [which] began almost immediately after Whitney's [cotton gin] was put to work', and which quickly became, concludes Basalla, 'the point of origin for an entirely new set of artifacts'.[13]

Divergence prepares the ground for convergence, which unleashes further divergence: this seems to be the typical pattern.[14] Moreover, the force of the two mechanisms varies widely from field to field, ranging from the pole of technology, where convergence is particularly strong, to the opposite extreme of language, where divergence—remember the 'matrix of distances' of figure 2—is clearly the dominant factor; while the specific position of literature—this technology-of-language—within the whole spectrum remains to be determined.[15] And don't be misled by the 'topological' technicalities of all this: the real content of the controversy, not technical at all, is our very idea of culture. Because if the basic mechanism of change is that of divergence, then cultural history is bound to be random, full of false starts, and profoundly path-dependent: a direction, once taken, can seldom be reversed, and culture hardens into a true 'second nature'—hardly a benign metaphor. If, on the other hand, the basic mechanism is that of convergence, change will be frequent, fast, deliberate, reversible: culture becomes more plastic, more *human*, if you

---

[13] Basalla, *The Evolution of Technology*, pp. 30, 34.
[14] It is easy (in theory, at least) to apply this cyclical matrix to the history of genres: convergence among separate lineages would be decisive in the production of new genres; then, once a genre's form stabilizes, 'interbreeding' would stop, and divergence would become the dominant force.
[15] In Thomas Pavel's recent *La Pensée du Roman*, Paris 2003, which is the most ambitious theory of the novel since the masterpieces of the inter-war years, divergence is the fundamental force during the first seventeen centuries of the novel's existence, and convergence in the last three (these are my extrapolations, not Pavel's). The interpretation of these results is however far from obvious. Should one insist on the striking quantitative supremacy of divergence even in the notoriously 'synchretic' genre of the novel? Or should one focus on the (apparent) historical trend, viewing divergence as a 'primitive' morphological principle, and convergence as a more 'mature' one? And are Balzac, say, or Joyce, only instances of convergence (pp. 245, 373)—or are they also the initiators of strikingly new formal branches? All questions for another occasion.

wish. But as human history is so seldom human, this is perhaps not the strongest of arguments.

V

One last tree: this time, not the 'many more ways of being dead' of Conan Doyle's rivals, but the still numerous 'ways of being alive' discovered between 1800 and 2000 by that great narrative device known as 'free indirect style'. The technique was first noticed in an article on French grammar published in 1887 in the *Zeitschrift für romanische Philologie*, which described it, in passing, as 'a peculiar mix of indirect and direct discourse, which draws the verbal tenses and pronouns from the former, and the tone and the order of the sentence from the latter'.[16] *Mansfield Park*:

> It was the abode of noise, disorder, and impropriety. Nobody was in their right place, nothing was done as it ought to be. She could not respect her parents, as she had hoped.[17]

Nobody was *in their right place*, nothing was done *as it ought to be*: the tone is clearly Fanny's, and expresses her profound emotional frustration at her parents' house. Nobody *was* in their right place . . . *She could* not respect *her* parents: the (past) verbal tenses and (third person) pronouns evoke for their part the typical distance of narrative discourse. Emotions, plus distance: it is truly an odd *Mischung*, free indirect style, but its composite nature was precisely what made it 'click' with that other strange compromise formation which is the process of modern socialization: by leaving the individual voice a certain amount of freedom, while permeating it with the impersonal stance of the narrator, free indirect style enacted that *véritable transposition de l'objectif dans le subjectif*[18] which is indeed the substance of the socialization process. And the result was the genesis of an unprecedented 'third' voice, intermediate and almost neutral in tone between character and narrator: the composed, slightly abstract voice of the *well-socialized individual*, of which Austen's heroines—these

---

[16] A. Tobler, 'Vermischte Beiträge zur französischen Grammatik', *Zeitschrift für romanische Philologie*, 1887, p. 437.
[17] *Mansfield Park*, ch. 39.
[18] Charles Bally, 'Le style indirecte libre en français moderne', *Germanisch-Romanische Monatschrift*, 1912, second part, p. 603.

young women who speak of themselves *in the third person*, as if from the outside—are such stunning examples.[19]

Placed as it is halfway between social *doxa* and the individual voice, free indirect style is a good indicator of their changing balance of forces, of which the tree in figure 6 (overleaf) offers a schematic visualization. And as can be seen, not much happens as long as free indirect style remains confined to western Europe; at most, we have the gradual, entropic drift from 'reflective' to 'non-reflective' consciousness:[20] that is to say, from sharp punctual utterances like those in *Mansfield Park*, to Flaubert's and Zola's all-encompassing moods, where the character's inner space is unknowingly colonized by the commonplaces of public opinion. But just as the individual mind seems about to be submerged by ideology, a geographical shift to the east reverses the trend, associating free indirect style with conflict rather than with consensus. Raskolnikov's inner speech, writes Bakhtin

> is filled with other people's words that he has recently heard or read [and is] constructed like a succession of living and impassioned replies to all those words ... He does not think about phenomena, he speaks with them ... he addresses himself (often in the second person singular, as if to another person), he tries to persuade himself, he taunts, exposes, ridicules himself[21]

A language filled with 'other people's words', just like Emma Bovary's: but where those words, instead of being passively echoed, arouse 'living and impassioned replies'. Here are Raskolnikov's reactions to the news of his sister's impending (and loveless) marriage:

> 'Won't take place? And what are you going to do to stop it? Forbid it? By what right? What can you promise them instead, in order to possess such a right?

---

[19] I have analyzed in detail the connexion between free indirect style and socialization in 'Il secolo serio', *Il romanzo*, vol. I, Torino 2001 (forthcoming, Princeton 2005). Needless to say, I do not claim that free indirect style is *only* used to represent the process of socialization (which would be absurd), but rather that between the two existed—especially early on—a profound elective affinity.

[20] For these terms, see Ann Banfield's classic study of free indirect style, *Unspeakable Sentences*, Boston 1982.

[21] Mikhail Bakhtin, *Problems of Dostoevsky's Poetics*, 1929–63, Minneapolis 1984, pp. 237–8. The dialogic reinterpretation of free indirect style sketched by Bakhtin is extensively developed in Volosinov's chapters on 'quasi-direct discourse' in *Marxism and the Philosophy of Language* [1929], Cambridge, MA 1993, pp. 125–59; see also Gary Morson and Caryl Emerson, *Mikhail Bakhtin. Creation of a Prosaics*, Palo Alto, CA 1990, esp. pp. 343–4.

FIGURE 6: *Free indirect style in modern narrative, 1800–2000*

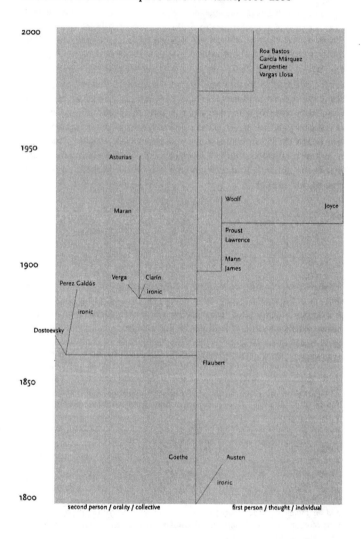

This figure reflects work in progress, and is therefore quite tentative, especially in the case of non-European literatures, and of the diachronic span of the various branches.

To devote your whole life, your whole future to them, *when you finish your course and get a job?* We've heard that one before, that's just maybe—what about *now?* I mean, you've got to do something right now, do you realize that?' . . . It was a long time since [these questions] had began to lacerate his heart, and it was positively an age since his present sense of anguish and depression had come into being . . . It was clear that now was not the time to feel miserable, to suffer passively with the thought that the questions were not capable of resolution; no, instead he must do something, and at once, as quickly as possible. Whatever happened, he must take some action, or else . . .'[22]

Great page. But can we really speak of free indirect style for those sentences in 'the second person singular, as if to another person' that open the passage, and that are so crucial for Bakhtin's argument (and for his entire theory of the novel)? No, not quite: the second person (especially if in quotes) indicates the *direct* discourse of an open-ended discussion, rather than (as in the second half of the passage) the *narrative* report of thoughts and emotions. Why this double register, then, why this shift in the representation of Raskolnikov's inner debate? Probably, what happened was something like this: entrusted by Dostoevsky with a dialogic task so unlike its usual one, the free indirect style of *Crime and Punishment* became more intense and dramatic ('he must take some action, or else') than ever before, 'stretching' as far as it possibly could; but in the end, the open-endedness of dialogism was incompatible with the narrative register of free indirect style, and so—in a little morphological 'catastrophe'—the latter's key traits were all rearranged according to a different logic. A border had been crossed, and free indirect style had 'mutated' into something else.

VI

Bakhtin's conceptual vocabulary, with its emphasis on the oral threads within novelistic prose, is a good prologue to the next branching of the tree, which occurs around 1880, at the height of the naturalist movement. Here, the fault line—which is, again, geographic and morphological at once—runs between different forms of symbolic hegemony in *fin-de-siècle* Europe: in the West, the silent, interiorized *doxa* of large nation-states, arising almost impersonally from newspapers, books, and

---

[22] *Crime and Punishment*, ch. 4.

an anonymous public opinion; in the South, the noisy, *multi*-personal 'chorus' (Leo Spitzer) of the small village of *I Malavoglia*, or the sharp whispers of the provincial confessionals of *La Regenta*; later, the *longue durée* of collective oral myths in *Batouala* or *Men of Maize*.[23] Here, free indirect style embodies a form of social cohesion which—in its reliance on explicit, *spoken* utterances, rather than 'non-reflective' absorption—is more quarrelsome and intrusive than in western Europe, but also much more unstable: the spokesmen for the social (villagers, confessor, chief) must be always *physically there*, ready to reiterate over and over again the dominant values, or else things fall apart. As indeed they do, in all of these novels.

So far, we have followed free indirect style as it explored the 'objective' pole of its tonal scale: the 'truths' of the neo-classical narrator and the *doxa* of public opinion; the force (in Dostoevsky) of abstract theories and ideas, and the myths of traditional societies. Around 1900, however, a different group of writers begins to experiment at the opposite end of the spectrum, that of the irreducibly singular. First comes a cluster of upper-class stylizations (James, Mann, Proust, Woolf . . .), where the deviation from social norms is often so slight that it may not even form a separate branch; then, more decisively, Joyce's generation moves well beyond 'non-reflective consciousness', into the pre-, or un-conscious layers of psychic life. And at this point, a second stylistic 'catastrophe' occurs: just as, in *Crime and Punishment*, the third person of narrative discourse was taking turns with the second person of dialogue, in *Ulysses* it is constantly sliding into the *first* person of the stream of consciousness—with all the galaxy of idiosyncratic associations that this

---

[23] Two examples. 'Nowadays mischief-makers got up to all kinds of tricks; and at Trezza you saw faces which had never been seen there before, on the cliffs, people claiming to be going fishing, and they even stole the sheets put out to dry, if there happened to be any. Poor Nunziata had had a new sheet stolen that way. Poor girl! Imagine robbing her, a girl who had worked her fingers to the bone to provide bread for all those little brothers her father had left on her hands when he had upped and gone to seek his fortune in Alexandria of Egypt.' Giovanni Verga, *I Malavoglia*, ch. 2.

'He's a good old man, the sun, and so equitable! He shines for all living people, from the greatest to the most humble. He knows neither rich nor poor, neither black nor white. Whatever may be their colour, whatever may be their fortune, all men are his sons. He loves them all equally; favours their plantations; dispels, to please them, the cold and sullen fog; reabsorbs the rain; and drives out the shadow. Ah! The shadow. Unpityingly, relentlessly, the sun pursues it wherever it may be. He hates nothing else.' René Maran, *Batouala*, ch. 8.

technique entails.[24] And through the prism of this small grammatical shift, one can again glimpse a branching process of a higher order, where psychological realism 'speciates' into modernist epics, just as, earlier, it had metamorphosed into dialogic novels.

In the final branching of the tree—Latin American 'dictator novels'—the fluctuation between third and first person is still there, but its direction has been reversed: in place of a third person narrative modulating into a first person monologue, we see the dictator's attempt to objectify his private (and pathological) self into the monumental poses of a public persona. 'My dynasty begins and ends in me, in I-HE,' writes Augusto Roa Bastos in *I the Supreme*; and towards the end of the book:

> HE, erect, with his usual brio, the sovereign power of his first day. One hand behind him, the other tucked in the lapel of his frock coat . . . I is HE, definitively, I-HE-SUPREME. Immemorial. Imperishable.[25]

In Roa Bastos' novel, as in Carpentier's *Reasons of State* and García Márquez's *General in his Labyrinth*—the other two dictator novels of 1974, a year after the *putsch* against Allende in Chile—the 'I' of El Supremo still largely overshadows his 'HE', thus confining free indirect style to quite a limited role. But with Mario Vargas Llosa the technique moves into the foreground, and realizes its full political potential: by presenting the mind of the dictator 'unmediated by any judging point of view'—to repeat Ann Banfield's limpid definition of free indirect style[26]—Vargas Llosa endows the putrid substratum of political terror with an unforgettably sinister matter-of-factness:

> Had the United States had a more sincere friend than him, in the past thirty-one years? What government had given them greater support in the UN? Which was the first to declare war on Germany and Japan? Who gave the biggest bribes to representatives, senators, governors, mayors, lawyers and reporters in the United States? His reward: economic sanctions by the OAS to make that nigger Rómulo Betancourt happy, to keep sucking at the tit of the Venezuelan oil. If Johnny Abbes had handled things better and the bomb had blown off the head of that faggot Rómulo, there wouldn't be any

---

[24] 'He looked down at the boots he had blacked and polished. She had outlived him. Lost her husband. More dead for her than for me. One must outlive the other. Wise men say. There are more women than men in the world. Condole with her. Your terrible loss. I hope you'll soon follow him. For hindu widows only. She would marry another. Him? No. Yet who knows after.' James Joyce, *Ulysses*, ch. 6.

[25] Roa Bastos, *I the Supreme*, Normal, IL 2000, pp. 123, 419.

[26] Ann Banfield, *Unspeakable Sentences*, Boston 1982, p. 97.

sanctions and the asshole gringos wouldn't be handing him bullshit about
sovereignty, democracy, and human rights.[27]

VII

From the abode of noise and impropriety, where nobody was in their
right place, to the asshole gringos handing him bullshit about sovereignty, democracy, and human rights. This is what comparative literature
could be, if it took itself seriously as *world literature*, on the one hand,
and as *comparative morphology*, on the other. Take a form, follow it from
space to space, and study the reasons for its transformations: the 'oppor-
tunistic, hence unpredictable' reasons of evolution, in Ernst Mayr's
words.[28] And of course the multiplicity of spaces is the great challenge,
and the curse, almost, of comparative literature: but it is also its peculiar
strength, because it is only in such a wide, non-homogeneous geography
that some fundamental principles of cultural history become manifest.
As, here, the dependence of morphological novelty on spatial discontinuity: 'allopatric speciation', to quote Ernst Mayr one more time: a new
species (or at any rate a new formal arrangement), arising when a population migrates into a new homeland, and must quickly change in order
to survive. Just like free indirect style when it moves into Petersburg,
Aci Trezza, Dublin, Ciudad Trujillo . . .

Spatial discontinuity boosting morphological divergence. It's a situation
that reminds me of Gide's reflections on the form of the novel at the
time he was writing *The Counterfeiters*: granted that the novel is a slice
of life, he muses, why should we always slice 'in the direction of length',
emphasizing the passage of time? why not slice *in the direction of width*,
and of the multiplicity of simultaneous events? Length, plus width: this
is how a tree signifies. And you look at figure 6, or at the others before it,
and cannot help but wonder: which is the most significant axis, here—
the vertical, or the horizontal? diachronic succession, or synchronic
drifting apart? This perceptual uncertainty between history and form—
this impossibility, in fact, of really 'seeing' them both at once—is the
result of a new conception of literary history, in which literature moves
forwards *and sideways* at once; often, more sideways than forwards. Like
Shklovsky's great metaphor for art, the knight's move at chess.

---

[27] Vargas Llosa, *The Feast of the Goat*, ch. 2.
[28] Mayr, *Toward a new Philosophy of Biology*, p. 458.

VIII

Three articles; three models; three snapshots of the literary field: first the system as a whole, then the middle ground of chronotopes and genres, and now the micro-level of stylistic devices. But despite the difference of scale, some constants remain. First, a total indifference to the philosophizing that goes by the name of 'Theory' in literature departments. It is precisely *in the name of theoretical knowledge* that 'Theory' should be forgotten, and replaced with the extraordinary array of conceptual constructions—theories, plural, and with a lower case 't'—developed by the natural and by the social sciences. 'Theories are nets', wrote Novalis, 'and only he who casts will catch'. Theories are nets, and we should learn to evaluate them for the empirical data they allow us to process and understand: for how they *concretely change the way we work*, rather than as ends in themselves. Theories are nets; and there are so many interesting creatures that await to be caught, if only we try.

Finally, the approaches I have discussed (and others that could have been added) also share a clear preference *for explanation over interpretation*. They don't offer a new reading of *Waverley*, *Black Forest Village Stories*, or *I Malavoglia*, but aim to understand the larger structures within which these have a meaning in the first place: the temporal cycles which determine the coming and going of genres, or the circular patterns typical of old village culture, or the stylistic branches that delimit the social function of free indirect style. Were I to name a common denominator for all these attempts, I would probably choose: *a materialist conception of form*. An echo of the Marxist problematic of the 1960s and 70s? Yes and no. Yes, because the great idea of that critical season—form as the most profoundly social aspect of literature: *form as force*, as I put it in the close to my previous article—remains for me as valid as ever. And no, because I no longer believe that a single explanatory framework may account for the many levels of literary production and their multiple links with the larger social system: whence the conceptual eclecticism of these articles, and the tentative nature of many of the examples. Much remains to be done, of course, on the compatibility of the various models, and the explanatory hierarchy to be established among them. But right now, opening new conceptual possibilities seemed more important than justifying them in every detail.

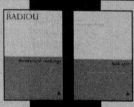

ÇAĞLAR KEYDER

THE TURKISH BELL JAR

THE SUMMER OF 2004 has seen a new sense of optimism in Turkey. A stable government has garnered a series of successes both in legislating democratic reforms and in international diplomacy. Long-promised rights and safeguards have been put in place, significantly reducing the authoritarian legacy of the republican state. The EU announced that the country had fulfilled its requirements for political reform, and no longer had to be monitored. It is widely expected that negotiations for membership to the EU will be given the go-ahead later this year and that foreign capital may start to flow in. Inflation has been reduced and the economy is currently in an upswing, registering a growth rate above 10 per cent last quarter. Yet, barely three years ago, Turkey's political instability—erupting in a public row between president and prime minister—catalysed a financial crisis, with a 50 per cent devaluation of the currency, severe recession and soaring unemployment. A year later, in summer 2002, the coalition government (Turkey's seventh in a decade) collapsed in disarray. The political and economic outcomes of these debacles unfolded within the context of the Iraq War and US-led occupation, EU pressures to reform the highly authoritarian state system, electoral breakthrough by the populist Islamist AKP and intensified IMF-led restructuring.

The 2001 crisis itself represented the collapse of a two-decade attempt by Turkey's traditional elite to shore up its faltering ideological hold through resort to state coercion. The state is a concept with an unequivocal referent in the Turkish context. In its eyes, the nation is an organic totality whose true interests can be known and fostered only by the Kemalist governing elite. It calls for constant vigilance against the forces who would dismantle the country and threaten Turkish national unity. The hegemony of the elite was established through the construction of the nation-state from the ashes of the Ottoman defeat, and sustained through the ordinary apparatuses of school and barracks. It was perpetuated through its control over foreign exchange and credit during the three decades of developmentalism that followed the Second World War. The state's arsenal of policies and resources dominated a weak bourgeoisie and moulded the largest businessmen into a willing alliance around a strategy of centrally coordinated national development on the import-substitution model.

As in Latin America, development came to an end due to an inability to perpetuate a largely closed economy. The crisis was occasioned by problems in securing foreign exchange. Urbanization and industrialization had ensured that most of the basic consumption items, durable goods included, were manufactured domestically. The Turkish economy produced a sufficient quantity of the staples, such as steel and petrochemicals. Yet none of these sectors could hope to compete in the world market. State enterprises were burdened with excessive employment, while in the private sector, monopoly positions translated to high profits and high wages. Despite a respectable growth performance, the economy could not generate the foreign-exchange earnings that were needed for essential imports such as oil and new technology.

The response of the Turkish political establishment in the 1970s was to perpetuate national-developmentalist rhetoric, borrow dollars abroad, and continue to protect industry, support agriculture and subsidize consumers. They attempted to control the market by fiat, setting exchange rates and prices at artificial levels, and watched helplessly as shortages grew and a black market flourished. The economic crisis and the social dislocation it instigated fuelled the already raging political struggle between the hardline right and the revolutionary left. The 1980 military coup was thus a response to the economic impasse as well as to political crisis. It ushered in a regime of exception under which the alliance of statist and authoritarian interests succeeded in stalling all attempts to break through its own fog of nationalist ideology.

The chief institutional legacy of the three years of overt military tutelage (1980–83) was the 1982 Constitution. Under this basic law, the powers of a National Security Council (NSC) were expanded to form what amounted to a parallel government, while the State Security Courts became a parallel legal system with jurisdiction over 'crimes against the state'. Within the NSC, military chiefs of staff met with top cabinet members and dictated the policies to be followed. The NSC was endowed with

a permanent secretariat and staff, designed to pool all intelligence and
to develop policy to be implemented by the relevant bureaucracy, often
bypassing the politically appointed ministers.[1] It gradually extended its
authority to cover any issue that could be deemed important in the total
war against separatism and the Islamic movement. A Higher Education
Council was established to oversee the universities, their personnel and
syllabuses, and a similar body to regulate the content of all broadcast
media. Virtually everything, from foreign and military policy to the
structure of civil and political rights, from secondary-school curricula
to energy policy, was eventually decided in the monthly meetings of the
NSC, invariably along the lines formulated by its secretariat. The civilian
governments that subsequently entered office, beginning with Turgut
Özal's election victory in 1983, essentially concerned themselves with
economic policy and the management of the debt. Meanwhile, the State
Security Courts served as unabashed organs of the 'deep state': their
jurisdiction extended to everything political, ranging from human rights
to anything that the state construed as separatist propaganda, within
which rubric even singing a song in Kurdish could qualify.[2]

Economic restructuring

Under the military-NSC regime, a radical makeover of the economy could
be embarked upon with minimum resistance. The gradual dismantle-
ment of the import-substituting industrial sector took place against a
backdrop of worsening income distribution. The share of wages and
salaries in national income dropped from around 30 per cent in the
1970s to roughly 20 per cent in the 1980s. Wages in manufacturing
had increased, more or less in line with productivity, over the three decades after 1950; by contrast, the level of real wages remained in 2000
what it had been in 1980, having dropped below that for long periods
in between. Manufacturing employment in the public sector fell from
250,000 to 100,000 between 1980 and 2000, due to downsizing and
privatization. Workers in the state-owned industries had constituted the
core of the labour movement of the 1960s and 70s—organized trade
unionists who received relatively high wages and good benefits. With

[1] The real status of the NSC emerged during the course of the war against the Kurdish
population in the Southeast: the administration of the war region and all matters of
free speech and exercise of rights connected to the Kurdish problem and ethnic matters came under the NSC's de facto authority.
[2] 'Bir Zümre, Bir Parti, Türkiye'de Ordu', articles by Ömer Laçiner, Ahmet İnsel,
Tanil Bora and Gülay Günlük-Şenesen, special issue of *Birikim*, Aug–Sept, 2002.

privatization, deregulation and flexible employment, the advantages
they had enjoyed in a protected manufacturing sector rapidly eroded.
Subcontracting, the spread of smaller enterprises and piecework became
standard practices; especially as the service sector gained ground, informal and diversified conditions of work increased.[3]

At the same time, market liberalization unleashed entrepreneurial ener-
gies at every level; traders and merchants were suddenly permitted to
do things for which they would have served jail sentences a few years
earlier. The industrial structures of the developmentalist era had been
characterized by the oligopoly of a few multi-tentacled holding companies, through which the import-substituting bourgeoisie of Istanbul,
with their privileged access to policy makers in Ankara, had been able
to maintain an iron grip over the economy. With liberalization, a new
breed of entrepreneurs emerged who had to compete in globalized markets, and indexed their behaviour to commercial and consumer signals
rather than bureaucratic decisions; hence their dependence on policy was
less direct. As Turkish exports gravitated toward labour-intensive manufactures, a number of smaller Anatolian cities with craft traditions and
non-unionized workforces, where households could be incorporated in
subcontracting deals, began to emerge as regional industrial centres.[4]
Most of the production in these towns, the so-called Anatolian Tigers, was
located on buyer-driven networks: businessmen contracted directly with
retail chains and volume buyers in Europe. Dealings with the economic
bureaucracy of the state were considered a burden rather than a benefit.

The 1980s thus saw the emergence of new sectors, new markets, new
forms of labour organization and new geographies. Exports increased
from $3 billion in 1980 to $13 billion in 1990, and to $50 billion in
2003—the expansion entirely due to manufactures, especially textiles.
From Ankara's point of view, the new businessmen functioned outside
the customary networks of influence and privilege, and did not share
the westernized style and militant secularism of their more entrenched
counterparts in Istanbul; they were more likely to support an Islamic

---

[3] Today only five per cent of the labour force is unionized—barely one million, out
of over twenty million workers—within a highly fragmented institutional structure.
[4] See, for example, Asuman Türkün-Erendil, 'Mit ve Gerçeklik Olarak Denizli—
Üretim ve İşgücünün Değişen Yapısı', *Toplum ve Bilim*, no. 86, 2000. This pattern
well conforms with the expectations of post-Fordist theory: see Charles Sabel,
'Flexible Specialization and the Re-emergence of Regional Economies', in Ash
Amin, ed., *Post-Fordism*, Oxford 1994.

party, and to associate themselves with MÜSIAD, an association of Islamic businessmen, which became an important social and political counterweight to the association of Istanbul industrialists, TÜSIAD.[5]

Islamist movement

Opening to the world market and restructuring the economy depleted the resources that had served to purchase popular consent. The last two decades of Turkish history have been coloured by state forces attempting to find new ways of securing domination over a transformed and increasingly vocal society. Having lost the legitimacy accorded them during the developmentalist period, since 1980 they have relied heavily on various forms of coercion to maintain the statist equation in face of emerging forces that have sought to establish their own economic, cultural and political autonomy. The rise of the Islamist parties has posed a particular dilemma for the traditional ruling class. Secularism, defined as strict state control over religion, has been a principal concern of the Turkish elite since the inception of the republic. In their conception of modernization, western modes of conduct had to be adopted to replace local particularisms; Islam, of course, was the most blatant expression of the local. Furthermore, a fundamentalist interpretation of Islamic law conflicted with both the allegiance required by the state of its citizens, and with the unique legal system that Kemalism wished to impose. However, contradicting their vigilant rhetoric, republicans have in fact been pragmatic in their dealings with even the more extreme versions of religious affiliation; their secularism conceals an underlying hypocrisy toward Islam and Islamists. Starting in the 1940s, political parties bargained with the leaders of sects, granting concessions on religious schools in exchange for their devotees' votes. After the coup in 1980, the military junta subscribed uncritically to the American policy of encouraging Islamism as a buffer against the socialist movement.[6] With the

---

[5] Ayşe Buğra, 'Class, Culture, and State', *International Journal of Middle East Studies*, vol. 30, no. 4, 1998.

[6] During the Kurdish war, the 'deep state' contracted with a brutal extremist faction of Islamists, Hizbollah, to eliminate businessmen sympathising with the Kurdish side. Themselves mostly Kurds, Hizbollah were a fundamentalist Sunni faction, with no relation to the Shi'ite party of the same name. This patronage, it now appears, continued after hostilities ceased in the Southeast, facilitating Hizbollah's international mobility and alleged participation in the Istanbul suicide bombings of November 2003. The security force's pretence of being able to control the fundamentalists for its own purposes had backfired.

education system undermined by IMF fiscal austerity measures, enrolment in government-backed religious *lycées* grew faster than that in general secondary schools during the 1980s, and religion was made a compulsory element of the curriculum. During these years, party leaders competed for good relations with various moderate and modernist Islamic factions, Özal winning their support in 1983.

Since the mid-80s, Islamists have steadily increased their share of the vote. Under Necmettin Erbakan's leadership, the Islamist Refah (Welfare) Party won 8 per cent in 1987, 16 per cent in 1991 and 21 per cent in 1995. Observers of political Islam have argued that the fundamentalist platform, defined as a project to replace the modern state and western law with Islamic ones, appeals to no more than 6 or 7 per cent of the population. The much larger numbers that have voted for the Islamic parties have arguably done so not because they want an anti-secular systemic change but because they favour an opening, a widening of the base that the system acknowledges. Islam has served as a rallying cry for those who were forced to remain outside the imaginary city walls when large-scale urbanization started, for the smaller entrepreneurs against the state-supported bourgeoisie of Istanbul, for politicians who did not enjoy the military's stamp of approval.[7]

Earlier incarnations of Islamic parties—Refah, dissolved under pressure from the NSC in 1998, following its short-lived coalition government with Tansu Çiller's centre-right True Path (DYP), was replaced by Fazilet (Virtue), itself closed down in 2001—oscillated between defying the system and adapting to it, and failed to harness this populist impulse to a programme that would be politically acceptable to the Turkish elite. The 2001 split in the Islamist ranks after the Fazilet Party was banned saw the creation of the Adalet ve Kalkınma (Justice and Development) Party (AKP) led by Abdullah Gül and Tayyip Erdoğan, while the old guard around Erbakan set up the Saadet (Felicity) Party. The AKP successfully combined electoral rhetoric aimed at the excluded with a message to the elite that regime change was not on its agenda. In the November 2002

---

[7] There is a lot written on the Islamic movement in Turkey: Binnaz Toprak, *Islam and Political Development in Turkey*, Leiden 1981; Nilüfer Göle, *The Forbidden Modern: Civilization and Veiling*, Ann Arbor, MI 1996; Jenny White, *Islamist Mobilization in Turkey*, Seattle, WA 2002, are representative. Also see Haldun Gülalp, 'Globalization and Political Islam: The Social Bases of Turkey's Welfare Party', *International Journal of Middle East Studies*, vol. 33, no. 3, 2001.

elections the two Islamic parties received 37 per cent of the vote, with the AKP taking 34 per cent. The 10 per cent threshold imposed by the NSC's constitution duly disqualified all but one of the other parties, leaving the AKP with 60 per cent of the seats.[8]

The AKP's popular appeal is based on providing a voice to the heretofore excluded, while the validity of its material promises derives in large part from the local-government record of its precedent political formations, which succeeded in building a reputation for relative honesty in administrations customarily mired in corruption. These municipalities initiated social-assistance policies in an environment where there was virtually no government welfare policy targeting the poor, and where organized philanthropy was scant. They organized soup kitchens and health centres, offered in-kind aid to the destitute, and invariably set up social-assistance drives during Ramadan, pressuring local businessmen to donate goods, buildings and money. Such engagement involved large numbers of party activists (and especially young women) building networks and linking with the population. Tayyip Erdoğan himself, was the popular mayor of Istanbul from 1994 until his brief imprisonment in 1998. Islamist parties have thus been the principal conduit for the expression of economic resentment. Despite the AKP leaders' genuine commitment to neoliberal orthodoxy, and although they also articulate the aspirations and discontent of a rising Anatolian bourgeoisie as against the established business oligarchy, they receive the bulk of their votes from the poor. This support from the excluded is due more to the critique of the political system and its corruption than to explicit promises of economic restructuring or a rights-based social policy.

Kurdish questions

In addition to the Islamic movement, the issue that has occupied the Turkish agenda most consistently since 1980 has been the Kurdish problem. Any intimation of Kurdish or any other separatism was, of course, strictly forbidden at the foundation of the Republic, and the use of the Kurdish language in public speech or education has been rigidly outlawed ever since. Brutal cultural suppression combined with economic underdevelopment inevitably fed resistance. Martial law was continued in the

---

[8] The popular votes were 9.6 per cent for Çiller's True Path, 8.3 per cent for the Nationalists, 5.1 per cent for Motherland and 1.2 per cent for Ecevit.

Kurdish provinces after 1983, accompanied by mass arrests, torture and forcible relocation of villagers. In 1984 Abdullah Öcalan returned from Syrian exile to lead the Kurdish Workers' Party (PKK) in guerrilla attacks on the security forces. State repression was intensified in return: the war would claim 30,000 lives before it finally ended in 1999.

During the 1990s, the war against the Kurdish forces was used to jus- tify a gradual transition to a national security state, as the Army's chosen mode of response to the insurgency—military victory first, cultural freedoms later—gained the upper hand. The war allowed the return of the Rechtsstaat as the cloak under which a new era of repression and arbi- trary rule could flourish. The tentative openings created under Özal after 1983—expansions of the social sphere to acknowledge the hitherto taboo lifestyles that market liberalization fostered—shrank back. A military- dominated authoritarianism coupled with a lack of accountability characterized the decade. All attempts at democracy and the rule of law were brutally quashed in the name of national security.

The military justified its regency on the basis of the war, yet the war also compromised its standing. The 'special forces' had gained a particular reputation for brutality in their dealings with civilians. Much of the popula- tion left the war zone. In the mid-1990s more than 1,500 rural settlements were evacuated as part of the military campaign against guerrilla forces, leading to a massive displacement of Kurdish peasants. The area had become a separate jurisdiction, governed by a law of exception. Conscripts reported on their dehumanizing experience under arms.[9] There were well-documented cases of torture in prisons, and instances of the military and intelligence services using civilians to eliminate suspected support- ers of the PKK. As in similar cases elsewhere, funds for such clandestine activities were sometimes obtained through criminal means.

The military's strategy of defeating the guerrillas before there could be any talks on cultural and political rights would not have achieved its expen- sive success had a separatist platform enjoyed greater support. There

---

[9] Nadire Mater, *Mehmedin Kitabı: Güneydoğu'da Savaşmış Askerler Anlatıyor*, Istanbul 1999, was a milestone. See the review article by Ayşe Gül Altınay, '*Mehmedin Kitabı*: Challenging Narratives of War and Nationalism', *New Perspectives on Turkey*, no. 21, 1999. For a recent account see Hasan Cemal, *Kürtler*, Istanbul 2003; for a broader perspective Kemal Kirişci and Gareth Winrow, *The Kurdish Question and Turkey, an Example of a Trans-state Ethnic Conflict*, London 1997.

were historical and political reasons behind the PKK's failure. Under the Ottoman Empire, ethnicity—unlike religion or sect—had never been a barrier to assimilation or intermarriage. This legacy of ethnic neutrality has continued at the social level in modern Turkey, where the bourgeoisie and political-cultural elite derive from diverse backgrounds, and marriages bring together co-religionists of all ethnicities, including Kurds, Circassians, Albanians, Bosnians and recent converts to Islam. Assimilation has been the norm in the case of Kurds who have moved out of the Southeast and the East to western Turkey. Ethnic Kurds have long been prominent in politics, and were even over-represented in the parliament. The price of assimilation, however, was the suppression of ethnic identity. While in the Empire one could remain Kurdish and still become part of the Ottoman elite, in the Turkish nation-state Kurdishness, as all other ethnic allegiance, had to be a private affair; in public, all were Turks. Thus, while the politics of identity and cultural recognition would find a much wider appeal among Kurds living outside the region, separatism would not.

There are no reliable figures on the ethnic composition of the population in Turkey, since censuses assiduously avoid questions of ethnicity or native language. Best estimates suggest that the Kurdish population (defined variously) is between 10 to 20 per cent of the total, but intermarriage makes the count impossible. In 1990 perhaps a third of ethnic Kurds lived in the Western provinces of the country; in 2000, after ten years of war, the proportion had increased to 50 per cent. Istanbul is by far the largest Kurdish city, with more than one million Kurdish inhabitants. It would be difficult to find many proponents of a separatist movement subscribing to the goal of a landlocked Kurdistan among those living in western Turkey. Recent immigrants to Istanbul and the big cities of western Anatolia have been poor peasants, driven out of their villages, but with little desire to go back. In other words, most of the elite of Kurdish ethnic origin are not interested in a separatist solution, and it is unlikely that the subaltern Kurdish population, now making up a good proportion of the urban poor in large cities, will subscribe to any such movement.

There was an additional dimension which made it difficult for the Kurdish elite, rural or urban, to align with the nationalist movement. While earlier Kurdish insurrections of the 1920s and 1930s had originated within the landlord class and clergy, the modern movement was

rooted in the poor peasantry. The PKK started as an anti-feudal movement against Kurdish landlords in southeastern Turkey, who had been
the willing allies of the republican state in maintaining social control.
Elsewhere, the builders of the Turkish state had allied themselves with
the independent peasantry and even supported poor farmers in occupying land, but they had shied away from changing the social balance
in the Southeast. When the peasant movement started in the 1970s,
Ankara sent gendarmes to protect the landlords from the insurgen-
cies. This explains the 'socialism' of the PKK, its declared affinity with
movements such as the Shining Path, but also the lack of support for
the ideology and guerrilla tactics of the PKK and its commander Öcalan
among the Kurdish elite. Some clan chiefs continued to back Ankara
against the insurgents as the state recruited and armed a force of some
60,000 'village guards', themselves ethnic Kurds, who were supposed
to protect local populations against the guerrillas. Clashes were frequent
between the two, and the PKK's campaign to win over villagers sometimes degenerated into intimidation and massacres that almost took on
the appearance of a Kurdish civil war.

The UN Security Council passed its first resolution on the Kurdish
question in the aftermath of the Gulf War, with the creation of the US-
monitored no-fly zone in northern Iraq—thus officially putting the issue
of Kurds' human rights on the international agenda. In the same year,
Özal proposed a modification of the language ban to permit informal
speech. In 1993 Öcalan declared a ceasefire and renounced the demand
for an independent Kurdistan, instead claiming cultural and political
freedoms. Özal's sudden death put a halt to further negotiations, and
his successors moved swiftly to strengthen the army's presence in the
Southeast. The war was finally brought to an end in 1999. That February,
Öcalan was captured in Kenya, with Israeli and American help, flown
back to Turkey for a State Security Court trial and condemned to death.
In August, he called on the PKK to lay down its arms.

From Özal's death onwards there had been no suggestion from civilian politicians that there might be a non-military solution. The NSC
vetoed any attempts to broach the issue of cultural rights, although it
gradually became acceptable to talk about what was euphemistically
called 'the Kurdish reality'. Yet even such symbolic gains were due to
human-rights groups and journalists, rather than politicians. Against
the backdrop of war, the political parties mostly remained quiet—tacitly

accepting the military's strategy, without questioning the effects of the rigid imposition of national identity on the population. Highly central-ized inner-party regimes, with candidate lists drawn up by the leaders, assured block voting in the parliament. Ecevit's Democratic Left Party (DSP), dubbed a 'family partnership' in the press, was the most advanced in sycophancy. The far-right Nationalists (led by the veteran Turkes) were the more outspoken wing of the militarist camp, but Ecevit, with a simi-lar emphasis on the sanctity of the nation and its sovereignty, was at least as adamant in upholding the strictures of the 1982 Constitution. The Motherland Party (ANAP) of Mesut Yılmaz and the DYP were more in the nature of loose associations of interest without a stable political line. All participated in one or other of the short-lived coalition governments that characterized the 1990s, dutifully towing the line set out by the NSC; all fell below the 10 per cent mark in the November 2002 elections. Only the extraordinary conditions of civil war and ideological confinement, imposed by the military, could allow their corruption and ineptitude to go unscathed.

One function of the 10 per cent threshold was to ensure that the Kurdish movement would not be represented in parliament. When, in 1994, the Kurdish parties formed an electoral alliance with the centre-left and sailed over the mark, six deputies were arrested on charges of aiding the PKK; they remained in prison until June 2004. With the parliament becoming an increasingly irrelevant sideshow, real political debate over issues of democracy, ethnic representation and the effects of economic liberalization shifted to various extra-parliamentary forums: human-rights groups, the feminist movement, anti-war platforms, NGOS.

Debt crisis

In economic terms, too, the 1990s were Turkey's lost decade. Whereas growth had averaged 5.3 per cent during the 1980s, the economy shrank by 6 per cent in the crisis years of 1994 and 1999, and by 9 per cent in 2001. Investment fell, while bankruptcies and unemployment exploded. The average rate of inflation was around 80 per cent. Starting from manageable levels in the early 1990s, state indebtedness reached the alarming level of 150 per cent of GNP by 2001. With accumulation mounting every year, Turkey's entire tax revenue was required to serv-ice the debt; for the government to function beyond debt management, it had to have recourse to new loans. The level of debt accumulation has been due in large part to the excessively high interest rates paid to domestic lenders, averaging over 20 per cent in real terms for much of the 1990s. With lending to the government bringing such returns, investment in the real sector suffered. Banks bought the bonds issued by the Treasury and offered attractive rates to depositors. The bulk of the debt was held by a small group at the top of the concentration of wealth, who owned the high-interest deposits in the banks. In 2002, interest payments reached around 20 per cent of GNP, nine-tenths of it for internal debt. A century ago, Rosa Luxemburg described how the Ottoman state was employed as a tax-collecting conduit for the appropriation of surplus by international financiers; the present-day beneficiaries are a small group of local rentiers.

The state's systematic transferral of tax revenues to a rentier class was bound to create resentment among the 'active and working elements' in the real economy.[10] Not only did they suffer a worsening income distribution, they were also deprived of public-sector expenditures due to fiscal exhaustion. The debt economy introduced another distortion in the form of the unusual profitability of financial activity, consisting mostly of transactions in government bonds. Banks would borrow in foreign markets to buy state debt, gambling on the differential between the interest rate and the depreciation of the Turkish lira. Domestic savers and investors maintained holdings in local and foreign currency, buying and selling according to their expectations. The ensuing volatility encouraged further speculation. In this frenzied contest over the division of the spoils, the financial sector collected high returns from mediation, and invited corruption, political meddling and cronyism. There was also a high incidence of cross-investment between the financial sector and influential media: publishers could leverage their influence to buy banks, and bankers safeguarded their position by acquiring media. The biggest incidents of corruption involved politicians in league with bank owners plundering the state treasury.

Meanwhile successive governments found themselves squeezed for funds. As neoliberal globalization made deeper inroads, the political class was unable to offer any protection to the population against the ravages of market forces. Instead of engaging in politically unpopular

---

[10] Sentiments expressed by Keynes, quoted in Yılmaz Akyüz and Korkut Boratav, 'The Making of the Turkish Financial Crisis', Discussion Paper no. 158, UNCTAD, 2002. Also see Erinç Yeldan, *Küreselleşme Sürecinde Türkiye Ekonomisi*, Istanbul 2001.

tax reform, they restricted all expenditures in line with IMF prescriptions. Thus public education and health services were left to deteriorate (by 2000, social expenditures on health and education had decreased to 3.5 and 2.2 per cent of GNP respectively). Nationally owned companies were privatized, consumer subsidies were discontinued and agricultural support reduced. Public investment dried up and no further social assistance measures were put in place, despite the widely perceived ravages of new poverty. Turkey's rank in human development reports is 85, well below its GDP per capita ranking.

Into Europe?

Perhaps the major determinant of the domestic political scene in recent years has been Turkey's candidacy for the European Union—arguably, the only national project to enjoy popular support. This has not always been the case. In 1987, when Özal first applied for full membership, both the Islamic and the nationalist political forces were staunchly against a closer association with Europe, and what remained of the left had not yet totally outgrown its fascination with third-worldism. Despite the relaxation of statist control over the economy, Turkey's coddled bourgeoisie, fearing the loss of cozy profits from a protected market and state subsidies, was yet far from charting an independent course. In the 1990s, this began to change. A burgeoning urban middle class was growing impatient with official constructions of national identity, as propagated by the authors of the modernization project. Elements within the intelligentsia began to question the basic premises of statist developmentalism. Where previously political debate had been defined along a left-right continuum, the opposition's platform now focused increasingly on civil rights. Candidacy to the European Union became a crucial card to play at this juncture. Aware that they had neither the resources nor the ability to mobilize social forces to defeat the state, opposition groups came to see the candidacy process as the only way of winning support for greater democracy, rule of law and an expanded pluralism, as depicted in the Copenhagen criteria. By the end of the decade, the moderate wings of Islamic and Kurdish movements had joined the ranks of civil-society and human-rights activists advocating rapid fulfilment of the conditions required by Brussels.

The EU had in fact acquired a major presence in Turkey by the late 1990s. Euro-parliamentarians regularly visited areas of conflict, inspected prisons and gave overt support to human-rights organizations. The EU office in Ankara funded projects with the objective of strengthening civil society; contacts were established through NGO activities, ranging from working with homeless children to sponsoring environmental activists. Official visits served to remind the public that this special relationship continued on course. Almost imperceptibly, the EU had become a player in Turkish politics and public opinion. The country's heretofore insular political scene had been penetrated by new Europe-centred networks into which NGOs, political parties and state agencies found themselves drawn.

In addition, the Istanbul big bourgeoisie now swung their weight behind the EU project. Although Özal's 1987 membership application had met with rebuttal by the Commission—its reply, in 1989, had cited doubts about enlargement as well as the protectionism and imbalances of the Turkish economy—it had instead proposed a free-trade customs union, to come into force from 1995. Initially, the free-trade agreement was met with suspicion by some of Turkey's larger, first-generation industrialists. Having made their fortunes through protectionism, they were wary of unbridled competition. For many of the smaller, export-oriented businessmen, however, the Customs Union not only promised markets but also signalled the hope of keeping the capricious ministries and the planning authority out of their affairs. The struggle over the signing of the agreement was an important threshold, after which the bourgeoisie were left with no choice but to compete in larger markets. Their objectives therefore shifted to rationalization of the economic environment, and to curbing the state's arbitrary prerogatives. By the mid-1990s both TÜSIAD and the new Anatolian bourgeoisie had adopted a platform of democratization and reform, pursuing a relatively consistent programme of economic and political liberalization.[11]

To this end, TÜSIAD invited prominent academics to draft reform proposals to the Constitution, the judiciary and the electoral system; they

---

[11] Ziya Öniş and Umut Türem, 'Business, Globalization and Democracy: A Comparative Analysis of Turkish Business Associations', *Turkish Studies*, vol. 2, no. 2, 2001. For the history of the relations between Turkey and the EU, see Meltem Müftüler-Bac, *Turkey's relations with a changing Europe*, Manchester 1997; Mehmet Ugur, 'The Anchor-Credibility Problem in EU–Turkey Relations', in Jackie Gower and John Redmond, eds, *Enlarging the European Union*, Aldershot 2000; Birol Yesilada, 'Turkey's Candidacy for EU Membership', *Middle East Journal*, vol. 56, no. 1, 2002.

published position papers on the Kurdish situation, education, human rights and democratization. Although they were less than heroic in defending their positions against displeased representatives of the state, their timid attempts at a belated platform of bourgeois freedoms played an important role in legitimizing discussion on these issues. The salient point in these developments was that both Anatolian and Istanbul businessmen agreed that it was necessary to curb the excessive powers of the state. The lack of political will to introduce radical remedies and the unconcealed enthusiasm for graft had made Ankara an excrescence difficult for them to tolerate.

What made the opposition of the 'civil society' to continuing statist prerogatives possible was that the state elite and establishment politicians never faltered in their professed commitment to the European ideal. At the EU's 1997 'enlargement' summit in Luxemburg, Turkey's candidacy was consigned to deep freeze, but a withdrawal of the application was never mooted. Instead, the governing class seemed satisfied with the stand-off whereby Turkey would be seen as a perpetual supplicant for membership and the EU as a fickle and ultimately disinterested object of desire. This official pro-Europeanism made an appeal to the democratic norms required for EU candidacy a legitimate form of critique—the only one available, in fact, to those advocating greater civil liberties. To call for a rapid fulfillment of the EU conditions was a far safer option than direct confrontation with the formidable powers of the governing elite. Public opinion polls indicated a solid majority, between 65 and 75 per cent, behind this broad coalition of interests—even if this did not reflect a clear understanding of what EU membership would actually entail.

The unexpected development at this juncture was the switch in the EU's stance. In December 1999, two years after the Luxemburg rejection, the EU heads of state at the Helsinki summit meeting agreed to accept Turkey's candidate status. Observers have pointed to a number of factors. In Germany, Schroeder had replaced the more intransigent Kohl in 1998. Öcalan's imprisonment and the PKK surrender had defused the Kurdish issue. The Blair government had campaigned hard for enlargement as an antidote to integration. There was a new rapprochement with Greece, partly as a result of the 'earthquake diplomacy' of 1999. TÜSIAD had been lobbying successfully in Brussels. American support—in particular, Clinton's efforts at the OSCE summit in Istanbul in November 1999—was also seen as instrumental in securing the positive outcome at

Helsinki, although the US's frequent interventions in favour of Turkey's accession have been resented by Brussels, especially since G. W. Bush's presidency. Of course, Turkey had proved a loyal asset in the post-Cold War period, and entry into the EU, it was argued, would help to stabilize Turkey domestically, at no cost to the US and the 'western alliance'.

Nevertheless, the EU's 1999 decision to extend candidate status to Turkey took fractions of the state elite in Ankara by surprise. Having counted on perpetual postponement, they now found that the reforms suddenly demanded of them required significant alterations to their national-security system and its ideological props. The ideal of nation as community would have to yield to rule of law; enforcement of civil and political liberties would strengthen oppositional forces. The cultural rights of the Kurdish minority would have to be recognized, and secularism redefined to allow freedom of religious organization and expression. Perhaps most controversial, the military would have to abdicate its regency over the state. Accordingly, opposition to the European project, especially from the military but also from within the ranks of the bureaucracy and the judiciary, was openly voiced for the first time. Top generals opined that the EU, using the pretext of cultural rights, wanted to divide Turkey along ethnic lines; the far-right Nationalist Action Party, a member of Ecevit's coalition, was mobilized to defend the unitary national structure against European demands. Anti-EU forces pointed out that Turkey's geostrategic centrality meant it could always depend on IMF bail-outs and Washington's support. While the EU had initially been a state project for Turkey's elite, now it had become a platform for those who wanted to rein in the elite authoritarianism of Ankara. Rhetorical entrapment of the statist party served the democratizers well during the debate, however. Very few voices actually went so far as to propose a total rupture with the EU. Official Kemalist discourse would not permit such a jettisoning of the western ideal.

The unease of the military and their extensions in civilian government about the prospects of membership fed on the doubts of the European side. The dialogue between Turkey and the EU always hid more tension than the parties openly admitted to. European elites who aspired to a politically united federation objected to Turkey's membership on the same grounds that De Gaulle had opposed Britain's in the 1960s. Austrian and German Christian Democrats held that Turkey was not European enough, or too Islamic, culturally speaking. Opinion polls showed only minority support for Turkey's candidacy, though higher in Southern Europe than in the North. Giscard d'Estaing accused other politicians of hypocrisy, declaring that accepting Turkey into the Union would spell the end of Europe.[12] Yet the EU, too, was trapped in its own rhetoric as a 'union of the willing': ostensibly everyone who fulfilled the Copenhagen criteria could join. Hence, negotiations had to be allowed to proceed through the designated channels and bureaucratic momentum took over, with annual progress reports prepared by the Commission.

The AKP government

The pro-EU forces in Turkey were delivered an unexpected breakthrough with the AKP election victory in November 2002. Not only had the party actually promised to work for membership, but it was the only political force not compromised by its relationship with the state elite. Even before the government had been formed, Erdoğan started making the rounds of European capitals to garner support for Turkey's accession negotiations to be scheduled. It was the first time in fifteen years that an Ankara government had been formed by a single party, with a prime minister who could promise to implement reforms without fearing (or hiding behind) sabotage by coalition partners. Over the past eighteen months, the AKP government has worked feverishly to speed through the legislation begun under Ecevit. The prerogatives of the National Security Council have been reduced; it will be expanded to include a majority of civilians, one of whom will be its chairman. In June 2004 the imprisoned Kurdish deputies were finally released and a Kurdish-language programme, 'Our Cultural Riches', broadcast on state-run TRT. Other rights which will go some way toward satisfying the demands of the Kurdish minority may follow. It remains to be seen whether legislation to protect individuals against the coercive organs of the state has any effect on the actual behaviour of the police and courts. Torture and police brutality have long been staples of the Turkish state's relations with the populace, and civilian governments have lacked the courage

---

[12] Giscard d'Estaing and Helmut Schmidt co-authored a disapproving op-ed piece after the Helsinki summit where Turkey's candidacy was agreed. Giscard was particularly outspoken in November 2002 when he declared that Turkey was not a European country on account of geography and religion. See 'L'Europe sans frontières', *Le Monde*, November 9, 2002. Generally, Turkey's candidacy has been more popular among the left than the right (Britain is an exception), and in southern European countries more than in the North.

to bring the perpetrators to justice. Appeals by victims to the European Court of Human Rights have provided the only exceptions during the last decade, with the Turkish state ordered to pay damages to some of its own nationals. The AKP government has reiterated that ECHR decisions will be considered as case law by Turkish courts.

Erdoğan got a cool response on accession scheduling at the EU's Copenhagen summit in December 2002, at the height of the pre-Iraq War turbulence in trans-Atlantic relations. Turkey's case was postponed for consideration until December 2004. But the past year's insurgency in Iraq, as well as the AKP's confident progress, have led to a different emphasis. In May 2004, the EU's Commissioner for External Affairs, Chris Patten, described the December 2004 European Council vote as 'the main test of the European Union's commitment to a pluralist and inclusive approach to Islam'. In June, the Council announced that it was satisfied with Turkey's democratization and would stop monitoring its progress. Barring some major upset, it seems likely that December 2004 will see Turkey admitted to the EU waiting room, even if it has to remain there for a lengthy period while Brussels manoeuvres into place sufficient opt-outs, multi-tracks and subsidiarity loopholes to differentiate future farming subsidies and restrict the movement of new jobseekers.

Of course, beginning negotiations with the EU for eventual accession will not magically resolve the tensions Turkish social and political life engender. For the moment, the military seem resigned to the smaller role accorded them by Erdoğan's skillful manoeuvring, but calls for them to reassume the mantle of vigilant guardianship have not disappeared. The unfolding of the struggle will depend on AKP's success in negotiating the consent of its Islamic base toward a more centrist rule that will also satisfy the secularist establishment and the military. The role the military is likely to play also depends on how much the Turkish army will be committed to new wars and security undertakings planned by the Pentagon. The parliament veto of US troop transits through Turkey to Iraq in March 2003—one third of newly elected AKP deputies disobeyed the party whip to vote with the opposition Republican People's Party—seems unlikely to re-occur. The unheard-of act of Turkish disobedience caused fury in the White House, and Erdoğan has been trying hard to compensate ever since. By October 2003, he had managed to convince the AKP ranks to vote in favour of sending troops to support the US-led occupation, using the military's logic that an armed Turkish presence was necessary to prevent the formation of a Kurdish state. Only the urgent pleas of the Iraqi Governing Council prevented the deployment from taking place. The generals remain as important as ever to Washington, and Erdoğan himself committed to appeasing the US. It is not clear that the expanding professional stature of the army may easily be reconciled with a diminishing of its accustomed presence in political affairs—especially if there is a resurgence of Kurdish guerrilla activity within Turkey's borders.

On the fiscal front, the debt burden continues to increase and, even if the AKP succeeds in gradually lowering interest rates, the arithmetic seems unsustainable. The government is unlikely to declare outright bankruptcy in the near future, but once the atmosphere of perpetual crisis dispels, it will have to face growing resentment against austerity and the paucity of budget allocations to social expenditures. While economic recovery has been substantial since the crisis of 2001, Turkey's young and growing population sends a fresh contingent of young workers onto the job market each year, whose prospects in the age of jobless growth are increasingly disappointing. Labour-force restructuring has created a visible polarization in the big cities, which can no longer be remedied by the traditional mechanisms of large families and neighbourhood solidarity. During the 1990s, Kurds fleeing the war or forced out of the eastern and southeastern provinces predominated in the migration to the cities. While earlier arrivals were attracted by job opportunities or better access to education and health services, for the newcomers the decision is more likely to be based on sheer necessity. These displaced migrants have ended up in Istanbul, in shantytowns around Diyarbakır, Adana or Antalya, or in smaller towns along the coast. For most, there is no place to go back to.

The new urban poor have provided a vast pool of votes for the AKP, yet they remain an unpredictable factor. For the time being the AKP still benefits from its relatively clean past record on corruption. Its principal attraction for the urban poor lies not so much in concrete proposals as in its projection of empathy; it also profits from the absence of any alternative political channel for the expression of their discontent. Of the two major parties that claim a 'left' heritage, Ecevit's DSP had become ultra-nationalist and statist before its demise in the 2002 elections. The Republican People's Party, which now forms the parliamentary opposition with 19 per cent of the popular vote, defines itself primarily on the basis of its 'secularism'; accordingly most of its support derives from

the middle-class vote of the more developed regions and the larger cities. As the novelty wears off, the conflict between AKP's policies and the
demands of its principal constituency, emboldened by populist rhetoric,
will become increasingly tension-ridden. While some formal recognition by the EU of an eventual prospect of membership will provide a
definite boost, the future for Washington's 'beacon of democracy in the
Muslim world' still remains uncertain.

BENEDICT ANDERSON

IN THE WORLD-SHADOW

OF BISMARCK AND NOBEL

José Rizal: Paris, Havana, Barcelona, Berlin—2

N AN EARLIER article, 'Nitroglycerine in the Pomegranate' in NLR 27, I discussed the novels of Filipino José Rizal—*Noli me Tangere* and, in particular, *El Filibusterismo* (Subversion) of 1891—within a loosely literary framework. I argued that Rizal learnt much from European novelists, yet transformed what he found there to explosive new anticolonial effect. But Rizal was not only the first great novelist but also the founding father of the modern Philippine nation, and did not read merely fiction. He also perused the newspapers and magazines of the various capitals in which he lived—Madrid, Paris, Berlin, London— not to mention non-fiction books. More than that, from very early on his political trajectory was profoundly affected by events in Europe, the Caribbean, and elsewhere, and their often violent local backwash thousands of miles away in his home country. The aims of the present article are twofold. One is to use a transnational space/time framework to try to solve puzzles which have long perplexed critics of Rizal's last published novel. The second is to allow a new global landscape of the late nineteenth century to come into view, from the estranging vantage point of a brilliant young man (who coined the wonderful expression *el demonio de las comparaciones*) from one of its least-known peripheries.[1]

By the time *El Filibusterismo* was published in 1891, Rizal, now thirty, had been in Europe for almost ten years, and had learned the two master-languages of the subcontinent—German and French—as well as some English. He had also lived for extended periods in Paris, Berlin and London.

He subtitled his second major fiction *novela filipina* with good political reason. But it could almost as well be termed *novela mundial*. Bismarck had made Germany the dominant power in Europe, and pioneered a new global German imperialism (alongside several others, of course) in Africa, Asia and Oceania. Alfred Nobel had invented the first WMD readily available to energetic members of the oppressed classes almost anywhere. On the Left, the terrifying defeat of the Commune, the collapse of the First International, and Marx's death had opened the way for the rapid rise of anarchism in various forms, initially in France and Spain, but not much later in other parts of Europe, North America, the Caribbean and South America, as well as the Far East. I shall try to show how this global political context shaped the peculiar narrative of *El Filibusterismo*.

Compared to *Noli Me Tangere*, which has been translated into a good number of languages and is widely known and loved in the Philippines, *El Filibusterismo* is relatively unregarded. At one level, this neglect is easy to understand. The novel has no real hero. Women play no central role, and are barely sketched as characters. The plot and subplots are stories of failure, defeat, and death. The moral tone is darker, the politics more central, and the style more sardonic. One might say that if the Father of the Philippine Nation had not written it, the book would have had few readers up till today. For Filipino intellectuals and scholars it has been a puzzle, not least because they have been distressed by its apparent lack of verisimilitude, its non-correspondence with what is known about Philippine colonial society in the 1880s. The temptation therefore has been to analyse it in terms of its author's 'real-life' ambivalence on 'revolution' and political violence (which will be touched on later). But at least some of these difficulties are reduced if we consider the text as global, no less than local.

Shifts in Spain

In 1833 a dynastic crisis occurred in Spain, which gave rise to two successive civil wars, and haunted the country to the end of the century. In that year the ferociously reactionary Fernando VII—imprisoned and deposed by Napoleon, but restored by the Unholy Alliance in 1814—died, leaving

¹ I would like here to express my gratitude to Robin Blackburn and his student Evan Daniel, Carol Hau, Ambeth Ocampo, and Megan Thomas for all their help with material and criticism.

the crown to his only child, the three-year old Infanta Isabella, with her Neapolitan mother becoming Regent. Fernando's younger brother Carlos, however, disputed the succession, claiming that the 1830 public abrogation of the Salic law prohibiting women from becoming sovereigns was a manipulation designed to rob him of his inheritance. Raising an army in the ultraconservative North (Navarre, Aragon and the Basque country), he opened a war that lasted the rest of the decade and ended only in an uneasy truce. The Regent and her circle turned, for financial as well as political reasons, to the liberals for support; and, by a measure of far-reaching consequences, as we shall see, expropriated the property of all the powerful monastic Orders. At sixteen, Isabella was married off to the 'effeminate' Duke of Cádiz, and soon became accustomed to finding her pleasures elsewhere. On coming of age, she moved away from her mother's policies, fell under the sway of some ultraconservative clerics, and presided over an increasingly corrupt and ramshackle regime.

In the last months before this regime finally fell, in September 1868, Isabella ordered the deportation of a number of her republican enemies to the Philippines, where they were incarcerated on the fortified island of Corregidor in Manila Bay. In the empire-wide exhilaration that followed her abdication and flight to France, some older well-off, liberal-minded Manileño creoles and *mestizos*, including Antonio Maria Regidor, José Maria Basa and Joaquín Pardo de Tavera—later to become good friends of Rizal—organized a public subscription on behalf of the suffering prisoners.[2] In June 1869, the rich and liberal Andalusian General Carlos Maria de la Torre took over as the new 'Captain-General', and horrified much of the colonial elite by inviting creoles and *mestizos* into his palace to drink to 'Liberty', and strolling about the streets of Manila in everyday clothes. He then proceeded to abolish press censorship, encouraged freedom of speech and assembly, stopped flogging as a punishment in the military, and ended an agrarian revolt in Manila's neighbouring province of Cavite by pardoning the rebels and organizing them into a special police force.[3] The following year, Overseas Minister Segismundo Moret issued decrees putting the ancient Dominican University of Santo Tomás under state control, and encouraging friars to secularize themselves, while assuring them, if they did so, of continued control of their

---

[2] William Henry Scott, *The Unión Obrera Democrática: First Filipino Trade Union*, Quezon City 1992, pp. 6–7.
[3] Leon Ma. Guerrero, *The First Filipino: A Biography of José Rizal*, Manila 1991, pp. 9–11.

parishes in defiance of their religious superiors.⁴ The same exhilaration set off what became a ten-year insurrection in Cuba under the capable leadership of the well-to-do landowner Carlos Manuel de Céspedes, who at one point controlled the eastern half of the island.

But in Madrid, with the decision to install Amadeo of Savoy as the new (unpopular) sovereign, the political winds started to shift. In December 1870, Prime Minister General Juan Prim y Prats, who largely engineered Amadeo's accession, was assassinated; and thus, in April 1871, de la Torre was replaced by the conservative General Rafael de Izquierdo, Moret's decrees were suspended, and the new Captain-General abolished the traditional exemption from *corvée* labour for the Cavite naval shipyard workers. On February 20, 1872, a mutiny broke out in Cavite in which seven Spanish officers were killed. It was quickly suppressed, but Izquierdo followed up by arresting hundreds of creoles and *mestizos*— secular priests, merchants, lawyers, and even members of the colonial administration. Most of these people, including Basa, Regidor and Pardo Tavera, were eventually deported to the Marianas and beyond. But the regime, abetted by some conservative friars, decided to make a terrifying public example of three liberal, secular priests. After a brief kangaroo trial, the creoles José Burgos and Jacinto Zamora, and the aged Chinese *mestizo* Mariano Gómez, were garrotted in the presence of, it is said, forty thousand people. Rizal's beloved elder brother Paciano, who had been living in Burgos's house, was forced to go into hiding and forswear any further formal education.⁵

Six months later, on September 2, almost 1,200 workers in the Cavite shipyards and arsenal went on the first recorded strike in Philippine history. Numerous arrests and interrogations followed, but the regime failed to find an arrestable mastermind, and eventually all were released. William Henry Scott quotes Izquierdo's ruminations on this unpleasant surprise. Since 'more than a thousand men could not share exactly the same thoughts without some machiavellian leadership', the general concluded that 'the International has spread its black wings to cast its nefarious shadow over the most remote lands'. Unlikely as this perhaps sounds, the fact is that the International had only been banned by the Cortes at the end of 1871, and the Bakuninist Madrid section had made

⁴ John N. Schumacher, S. J., *The Propaganda Movement, 1880–1895* [rev. ed.], Quezon City 1997, p. 7.
⁵ Schumacher, *Propaganda Movement*, pp. 8–9; Guerrero, *First Filipino*, pp. 3–6, 13.

special mention in the maiden issue (January 15, 1870) of its official organ *La Solidaridad*, devoted to arousing the workers of the world, of 'Virgin Oceania and you who inhabit the rich, wide regions of Asia.'[6]

Student years

Many years afterward Rizal wrote that 'Had it not been for 1872, Rizal would now be a Jesuit, and instead of writing *Noli Me Tangere* would have written its opposite'.[7] With Paciano on the blacklist, Rizal's prime family name, Mercado, would have closed for little José any chance of a good education; he was therefore enrolled at the Ateneo under the secondary family name Rizal. In 1891, he dedicated *El Filibusterismo* to the memory of the three martyred priests. When asked, in 1887, by his Austrian friend, the ethnologist Ferdinand Blumentritt, what the meaning was of the odd word *filibustero*, he replied: 'The word *filibustero* is still very little known in the Philippines; the common people still are unaware of it. The first time I heard it [he was then eleven years old] was in 1872 when the executions took place. I still remember the terror it aroused. Our father forbade us ever to utter it ... [It means] a dangerous Patriot who will soon be hanged, or a presumptuous fellow'.[8] It turns out the word was coined around 1850 on one surprising shore of Céspedes's Caribbean, and from there drifted, via Cuba and Spain, across the Indian Ocean to Manila.[9]

---

[6] Scott, *Unión Obrera Democrática*, pp. 6–7.

[7] 'Sin 1872, Rizal sería ahora jesuita y en vez de escribir *Noli me tangere*, habría escrito lo contrario': Rizal's letter to his friend Mariano Ponce and staff members of *La Solidaridad*—1890s organ of the Filipino nationalists in Spain, as quoted in Guerrero, *First Filipino*, p. 608, note 13. My translation.

[8] 'Das Wort Filibustero ist noch auf den Philippinen sehr wenig bekannt worden; die niedrige Bevölkerung kennt es noch nicht. Als ich dieser Wort vom ersten Mal hörte, was es in 1872, wann die Hinrichtungen stattgefunden haben. Ich erinnere mich noch das Erschrecken welches dieser Wort weckte. Unser Vater hat uns verboten dieses Wort auszusprechen ... [It means] ein gefährlicher Patriote, welches in junger Zeit aufgehängt wird, oder ein eingebildeter Mensch!' *The Rizal–Blumentritt Correspondence*, Vol. 1, *1886–1889*, Manila 1992, fifth and sixth unnumbered pages after p. 65. Letter of March 29, 1887, from Berlin. My translation.

[9] F[ernando] Tárrida del Mármol, 'Aux Inquisiteurs d'Espagne', *La Revue Blanche*, vol. 12, no. 86 (1 February 1897), pp. 117–20. On p. 117 he wrote, of the *inquisiteurs modernes* in Spain, that 'their methods are always the same: torture, executions, slanders. If the wretched person whom they mean to destroy lives in Cuba, he is called a filibuster; if he lives in the Peninsula', an anarchist; if in the Philippines, a freemason [leurs procédés sont toujours les mêmes: la torture, les exécutions, les calomnies. Si le malheureux qu'ils veulent perdre demeure à Cuba, c'est un flibustier; si dans la péninsule, un anarchiste; si aux Philippines, un franc-maçon]'. We shall run into the

In the late spring of 1882, the 20-year-old Rizal left his country to study in Spain, concealing his plan from his parents, but supported by his elder brother Paciano and a sympathetic uncle. How was this possible? The Mercados were a cultivated, Spanish and Tagalog-speaking family of mixed 'Malay', Spanish, Chinese, and perhaps even remote Japanese descent. They were the most prosperous family in their town of Calamba (today an hour's drive south of Manila); but their wealth was also fragile, as they did not own much land, but rented it from the huge local Dominican *hacienda*. In 1882 world sugar prices were still high, but would crash in the depression that lasted from 1883 to 1886. The family would always send what money they could to José, but it was never enough, and the youngster was always hard put to make ends meet.

In any case, early in June, Rizal disembarked at Marseilles, before proceeding to Barcelona and on to Madrid to enrol as a student at Central University. The first disagreeable downward shock was, as he wrote to his family, 'I walked along those wide, clean streets, macadamized as in

---

redoubtable Tárrida later on. Suffice it here to say that he knew what he was talking about, since he was born in Cuba in 1861—the year also of Rizal's birth—and said of himself in the above article that *je suis cubain*.

In fact it appears that the word in its political, rather than older piratical ('freebooter'), meaning was coined in New Orleans around 1850. The local Francophone creoles and *mestizos* termed *filibustiers* the variegated idealists and mercenaries who joined the Venezuelan Narciso López in that city for three attempted invasions of Cuba (1849–51) to throw off its Spanish yoke. From creole, with its added 's', it must have passed into English and Spanish, since people like the notorious American mercenary William Walker, who made himself briefly president of Nicaragua in the mid-1850s, called themselves filibusters. Most likely, the carriers of the Spanish version to Manila were high-ranking Iberian military officers, many of whom served in the Caribbean before being sent to the Philippines. Four of the last five captain-generals in the archipelago, Valeriano Weyler (1888–91)—born to Prussian parents in Mallorca—Eulogio Despujol (1891–93), Ramón Blanco (1893–96) and Camilo Polavieja (1896–97) had all won their repressive spurs in the Caribbean, Despujol in Santo Domingo, the others in Cuba. Weyler would become world-notorious in the later 1890s when sent to Cuba to suppress the final nationalist insurrection. His policy of forced reconcentration of populations on a vast scale (prefiguring what the Americans did in Luzon in the 1900s) caused hundreds of thousands of deaths. It is a strange historical irony that López, who offered command of his second expedition to both Jefferson Davis and Robert E. Lee, was notorious for his 'severity' towards Blacks, allied himself with the Southern slavocracy, and recruited men mainly among veterans of the Mexican War, found posthumous 'patriotic' rehabilitation thanks to his public garrotting in Havana. The red-white-and-blue, star-and-stripes flag he designed for annexationist purposes remains Cuba's national flag today. See Hugh Thomas, *Cuba, The Pursuit of Freedom*, New Brunswick, NJ 1971, pp. 212–17.

Manila, crowded with people, attracting the attention of everyone; they called me Chinese, Japanese, American [i.e. Latin American], etc., but no one Filipino! Unfortunate country—no one knows a thing about you!'[10] In Madrid, he was to be asked by fellow students whether the Philippines was owned by the United Kingdom or by Spain, and another Filipino whether it was very far from Manila.[11] Yet the overwhelming Spanish ignorance of, and indifference to, his country was soon to have useful consequences. In the colony—but the Spanish state never called either the Philippines or Cuba a colony, and contained no Colonial Ministry— racial hierarchy, embedded in law, modes of taxation and sumptuary codes was of overriding importance to everyone. Peninsulars, creoles, Spanish and Chinese *mestizos*, 'Chinese', and *indios* were italicized social strata. In the Philippines, the word *filipino* referred to the creoles alone. In Spain, however, Rizal and his fellow students quickly discovered that these distinctions were either unknown or seen as irrelevant.[12] No mat- ter what their status was back home, here they were all *filipinos*, just as the Latin Americans in Madrid in the late eighteenth century were *americanos*, no matter if they were from Lima or Cartagena, or if they were creoles or of mixed ancestry.[13] (The same process has produced the contemporary American category 'Asians' and 'Asian Americans'.) On April 13, 1887, Rizal would write to Blumentritt that 'All of us have to make sacrifices for political purposes, even if we have no inclination to do so. This is understood by my friends, who publish our newspaper in Madrid; these friends are all youngsters, creoles, *mestizos* and Malays,

---

[10] 'Yo me paseaba por aquellas calles anchas y limpias adoquinadas como en Manila, llenas de gente, llamando la atención de todo el mundo, quienes me llamaban chino, japonés, americano, etc: ninguno filipino. Pobre país! Nadie tiene noticia de ti!' Letter of June 23, 1882 from Barcelona, in *One Hundred Letters of José Rizal*, Manila 1959, p. 26. These letters were not available when the big *Correspondencia Epistolar* was published.

[11] 'Que nos tomen por chinos, americanos o mulatos y muchos aun de los jóvenes estudiantes no saben si Filipinas perteniese a los ingleses o los españoles. Un día preguntaban a uno de nuestros paisanos si Filipinas estaba muy lejos de Manila.' Letter home from Madrid dated January 29, 1883, in *One Hundred Letters*, p. 85.

[12] In the first-class *Avant-Propos* she wrote to her new French translation of *Noli Me Tangere*, Jovita Ventura Castro noted that it was only after 1863 that students from the Philippines were permitted to enrol in metropolitan universities. (The translation, *N'y touchez pas!*, was published in Paris in 1980 by Gallimard with the sponsorship of UNESCO.) The first to enrol were creoles physically indistinguishable from Spain-born Spaniards. Multi-coloured *mestizos* and *indios* seem only to have arrived in the later 1870s. They were thus something visibly quite new.

[13] See my *Imagined Communities*, London 1991, p. 57.

[but] we call ourselves simply Filipinos.'[14] What they 'are' (colonially) is contrasted to what they 'call themselves' in the metropole. But there is actually a further elision, since many of these *mestizos* were 'Chinese' not 'Spanish'. (Indeed the Chinese *mestizos* vastly outnumbered their Spanish counterparts in the Philippines.)[15] The political *esfuerzo* involved probably explains why their newspaper called itself hopefully—and unmindful of the International—*La Solidaridad*. Thus one can suggest that Filipino nationalism really had its locational origins in urban Spain rather than in the Philippines.

For the next four years Rizal studied hard at Madrid's Central University. By the summer of 1885, he had received his doctorate in philosophy and letters, and would have done the same in medicine if his money had not run out. After Rizal's execution at the end of 1896, Miguel de Unamuno—who, though three years younger than the Filipino, entered the philosophy and letters faculty two years before him and graduated in 1884—claimed, perhaps truthfully, that he had 'seen him around' during those student days.[16] But for the purpose of this investigation, the most significant event occurred at the beginning of his senior year (1884–85) when Miguel Morayta, his history professor and a leading figure in Spanish Masonry, delivered an inaugural address that was a blistering attack on clerical obscurantism and an aggressive defence of academic freedom.[17] The scholar was promptly excommunicated by the

---

[14] 'Wir müssen alle der Politik etwas opfern, wenn auch wir keine Lust daran haben. Dies verstehen meine Freunde welche in Madrid unsere Zeitung herausgeben; diese Freunde sind alle Jünglingen, creolen, mestizen und malaien, wir nennen uns nur Philippiner.' See *Rizal–Blumentritt Correspondence, 1886–1889*, p. 72. It is important to recognize that the German word *Philippiner* is uncontaminated by the ambiguities surrounding *filipino*. It is clearly and simply (proto)national.

[15] It is very striking that the words *mestizo chino* do not occur in *Noli Me Tangere* at all, and only once, in passing, in *El Filibusterismo*. There are plenty of characters whom one can assume are such *mestizos*, but Rizal is careful not to mention their 'give-away' typical surnames. Sadly Iberian prejudices against the Chinese rubbed off rather heavily on the young anticolonial elite.

[16] Mentioned in the Mexican Leopoldo Zea's illuminating introduction to the Venezuelan edition of *Noli Me Tangere*, Caracas 1976, p. xviii, citing Unamuno's 'Epílogo' to W. E. Retana, *Vida y Escritos del Dr. José Rizal*, Madrid 1907.

[17] He particularly enraged the hierarchy by insisting that the *Rig Veda* was much older than the Old Testament, and that the Egyptians had pioneered the idea of retribution in the afterlife, and discussing in sceptical terms the Flood, and the Creation which even then Rome insisted had taken place in 4004 BC. Manuel Sarkisyanz, *Rizal and Republican Spain*, Manila 1995, p. 205.

Bishop of Avila and other mitre-wearers for heresy and besmirching
Spanish tradition and culture. The students went on a two-month strike
on Morayta's behalf, and were quickly supported by fellow students at
the big universities in Granada, Valencia, Oviedo, Seville, Valladolid,
Zaragoza, and Barcelona.[18] The government then sent the police in, and
many students were arrested and/or beaten up. Rizal later recalled that
he had only escaped arrest by hiding in Morayta's house, and assuming
three different disguises.[19] As we shall see later, this experience, transformed, became a key episode in the plot of *El Filibusterismo*.

There is only one other event from the student years that is here worth
underscoring: Rizal's first 'vacation' in Paris in the spring of 1883. We
described in 'Nitroglycerine in the Pomegranate' the excited letters he
wrote to his family from the French capital. There is nothing remotely
comparable for Madrid. Paris was the first geographical-political space
which allowed him to see Imperial Spain as profoundly backward—
economically, scientifically, industrially, educationally, culturally, and
politically.[20] This is one reason why his novels feel so unique among
anticolonial fictions written under colonialism. He was in a position to
ridicule the colonialists rather than merely to denounce them. He read
Eduard Douwes Dekker's *Max Havelaar* only after he had published *Noli
Me Tangere*, but one can see at once why he enjoyed the Dutchman's

[18] Rizal, *El Filibusterismo*, end notes, pp. 38–39. The editorial notes add that congratu-
lations and supportive protests came in from students in Bologna, Rome, Pisa,
Paris, Lisbon, Coimbra and various places in Germany.
[19] See the animated account Rizal gave his family in a letter of November 26, 1884,
in *One Hundred Letters*, pp. 197–200.
[20] According to the 1860 census, most of the adult working population was occu-
pationally distributed as follows: 2,345,000 rural labourers, 1,466,000 small
proprietors, 808,000 servants, 665,000 artisans, 333,000 small business-people,
262,000 indigents, 150,000 factory workers, 100,000 in the liberal professions
and related occupations, 70,000 'employees' (state functionaries?), 63,000 clergy
(including 20,000 women), and 23,000 miners. Jean Bécarud and Gilles Lapouge,
Anarchistes d'Espagne, Paris 1970, vol. I, pp. 14–15. Forty years later, in 1901, Barcelona
alone had 500,000 workers, but half of them were illiterate. See J. Romero Maura,
'Terrorism in Barcelona and Its Impact on Spanish Politics, 1904–1909', *Past and
Present* 41 (December 1968), p. 164. Schumacher goes so far as to claim a level of
equality in illiteracy between metropole and colony 'unique in the history of coloni-
zation'. (In 1900, illiteracy among people over ten years old in Spain was 58.7 per
cent; the American-organized census of 1903 showed a figure of 55.5 per cent for
the Philippines—this figure takes into account various local languages, Spanish,
and American). *The Propaganda Movement*, p. 304, fn. 9.

take-no-prisoners style of satire. In any case, by the time he graduated he had had enough of the metropole, and spent most of the next six years in 'advanced' Northern Europe. There are perhaps parallels with Martí, eight years older than Rizal, who studied in Spain in the mid-1870s, and then left it for good, spending much of the rest of his life in New York.

Imperial Europe

At this point we must temporarily leave 24-year-old Rizal in order to look schematically at the three worlds in which he found himself situated in the 1880s—the time of *Noli Me Tangere*'s publication and the planning of *El Filibusterismo*. One 'big world' was imperial Europe, and its American, Asian, and African peripheries. The central figure was certainly Bismarck. Having routed the armies of the Austro-Hungarian Empire at Königgrätz in 1866, he repeated this triumph in 1870 at Sedan, where Louis Napoleon and 100,000 French troops were forced to surrender. This victory made possible the proclamation, in January 1871—at Versailles, not Berlin—of the new German Empire, and the annexation of Alsace-Lorraine. After this, he began to interest himself in competing with Britain and France in extra-European imperial adventures—in East, Southwest and West Africa, in the Far East and in Oceania, particularly Spanish-claimed territories there. (We shall see the impact of this expansion when we return to Rizal, who liked Germany in part because it made Spain so paranoid.) Characteristically, the notorious carving up of Africa among the imperialists in 1878 was performed in Berlin. In dealing with Germany's well-organized working class and socialist party, Bismarck shrewdly combined repression with substantial social legislation. He remained in power till 1890, when the new, erratic Kaiser forced his resignation. *Noli Me Tangere*, a little incongruously, had appeared three years earlier in the imperial Hauptstadt.

In France, Bismarck's triumph at Sedan was followed by a brutal siege of Paris from which the shaky post-Louis Napoleon government had fled to Versailles, to sign there a humiliating armistice and later treaty. In March 1871 the Commune took power in the abandoned city and held it for two months. Then Versailles seized the moment to attack and, in one horrifying week, executed roughly 20,000 Communards or suspected sympathizers, a number higher than those killed in the recent war or during Robespierre's 'Terror' of 1793–94. More than 7,500 were jailed or deported to places like New Caledonia. Thousands of others fled to

Belgium, England, Italy, Spain and the United States. In 1872, stringent laws were passed that ruled out all possibilities of organizing on the left. Not till 1880 was there a general amnesty for exiled and imprisoned Communards. Meantime, the Third Republic found itself strong enough to renew and reinforce Louis Napoleon's imperialist expansion—in Indochina, Africa, and Oceania. Many of France's leading intellectuals and artists had participated in the Commune (Courbet was its quasi-minister of culture, Rimbaud and Pissarro were active propagandists) or were sympathetic to it.[21] The ferocious repression of 1871 and after was probably the key factor in alienating these milieux from the Third Republic and stirring their sympathy for its victims at home and abroad. We shall look more at this development later on.

Sedan also caused the withdrawal of the French garrison in Rome, and its replacement by the forces of the new, increasingly repressive and inefficient Kingdom of Italy. The Papacy, deprived of its temporal power, struck back politico-spiritually with the bizarre doctrine of Papal Infallibility, and threatened excommunication of any Catholic participating in the Kingdom's political institutions. Imperialism of a mediocre sort began in East Africa, while rural misery in the South was so great that between 1887 and 1900, half a million Italians left the country every year. Rizal visited Rome briefly in 1887 but seems not to have noticed anything but antiquities.

On his return to Europe in February 1888 via the Pacific, Rizal made a brief stop in mid-Meiji Japan, and was impressed by its orderliness, energy and ambition, and appalled by the rickshaws. It was gratifying, of course, to see a non-European people protect its independence and make rapid strides towards modernity. Though he spent a short time in Hong Kong, China itself seems to have been off his map. He reached San Francisco at election time, when anti-Asian demagogy was at its height. Enraged by being kept thirteen days on board ship for 'quarantine' purposes—the ship held about 650 Chinese—he hurried across the continent as rapidly as he could. Nothing would be less likely to impress him than the corruption of the Gilded Age, the post-Reconstruction repression of former Black slaves, the brutal anti-miscegenation laws and so on.[22] But he was

---

[21] See the vivid account and superb analysis in Kristin Ross, *The Emergence of Social Space: Rimbaud and the Paris Commune*, Minneapolis 1988; also James Joll, *The Anarchists*, Cambridge, MA 1980, pp. 148–49.

[22] See the concise account in Guerrero, *First Filipino*, p. 198.

already foreseeing American expansion across the Pacific. He then settled contentedly in London to do research on early Philippine history at the British Museum, and seems to have taken no interest in the gradually growing crisis over Ireland. (Living by Primrose Hill, was he aware that Engels was ensconced just round the corner?)

Anarchist stirrings

But this apparently calm world of conservative political dominance, capital accumulation and global imperialism was at the same time helping to create another kind of world, more directly related to Rizal's fiction. Indeed, already in 1883, he had sensed the direction of things to come:

> Europe constantly menaced by a terrifying conflagration; the sceptre of the world slipping from the trembling hands of declining France; the nations of the North preparing to seize it; Russia, over the head of whose emperor hangs the sword of Nihilism, like Damocles in Antiquity, such is Europe the Civilized.[23]

The year Rizal was born, Mikhail Bakunin escaped to Western Europe from Siberia where for a decade he had been serving a life-sentence for his conspiratorial activities against Tsardom in the 1840s. In 1862 Turgenev published *Fathers and Sons*, his masterly study of the outlook and psychology of a certain type of Nihilist. Four years later, a Moscow student named Karakozov attempted to shoot Alexander II, and was hanged with four others in the great public square of Smolensk.[24] That same year Alfred Nobel took out a patent on dynamite, which though based on highly unstable nitroglycerine, was both simple to use, fairly stable, and easily portable. In March 1869 the 22-year-old Sergei Nechayev left Russia and met Bakunin in Geneva, where they co-authored the sensational *Catechism of a Revolutionary*, then returned to Moscow a few months later. Bakunin kept up (strained) relations with the Nihilist

---

[23] 'Europa amenazada continuamente de una conflagración espantosa; el cetro del mundo que se escapia de las temblorosas manos de la Francia caduca; las naciones del Norte preparándose à recogerlo. Rusia cuya emperador tiene sobre sí la espada de Nihilismo como el antiguo Damocles, esto es Europa la civilizada . . .' Letter home from Madrid, dated October 28, 1883, in *One Hundred Letters*, p. 174. Spain seems not worth mentioning!
[24] For a *tableau vivant*, see Ramón Sempau, *Los Victimarios*, Barcelona 1901, p. 5. For an impressive listing, see Rafael Núñez Florencio, *El Terrorismo Anarquista, 1888–1909*, Madrid 1983, pp. 19–20.

leader despite the notorious murder of a sceptical student follower, later fictionalized by Dostoevsky in *The Possessed*.[25]

Towards the end of the 1870s, by which time the Nihilists had been succeeded by small clusters of Narodniki as the clandestine radical opposition to the autocracy, political assassination, successful and failed, had become quite common in Russia. 1878: in January, Vera Zasulich shot but failed to kill General Fyodor Trepov, military governor of St. Petersburg; in August Sergei Kravchinsky stabbed to death General Mezentsov, head of the Tsar's secret police. 1879: in February, Grigori Goldenberg shot to death the Governor of Kharkov, Prince Dmitri Kropotkin; in April a failed attempt by Alexander Soloviev to kill the Tsar in the same manner; in November Lev Hartmann's abortive try at mining the imperial railway carriage. 1880: Stepan Khalturin's successful blowing up of part of the Imperial Palace—8 dead, 45 wounded. Nobel's invention had now arrived politically. Then on March 1, 1881—15 months before Rizal landed in Marseilles—occurred the spectacular bomb-assassination of the Tsar, by the group calling itself Narodnaya Volya (The People's Will), that reverberated all over Europe.[26] (The assassination of US President Garfield a few months later was barely noticed.)

This particular form of political violence, targeted at heads of state, heads of governments, or powerful ministers, actually had its heyday from the late 1890s to the eve of the Great War, with Russia still setting the pace. There were many failed attempts (including one which cost Lenin's elder brother his life), but the list of successes seems today rather startling. French President Carnot (1894), Prime Minister Cánovas of Spain

---

[25] The *grouspuscule* was characteristically named The People's Retribution. Nechayev fled back to Switzerland, but was extradited in 1873, and sentenced to twenty years in prison. In 1882 he was 'found dead in his cell' *à la* Baader-Meinhof.

[26] Sempau, *Victimarios*, pp. 66–67; Norman Naimark, *Terrorists and Social Democrats, The Russian Revolutionary Movement under Alexander III*, Cambridge, MA 1983, ch. 1; Derek Offord, *The Russian revolutionary movement in the 1880s*, Cambridge 1986, ch. 1; and especially David Footman, *Red Prelude* [2nd ed.], London 1968. The first bomb failed to touch the Tsar. Realizing this, a figure whom Sempau names 'Miguel Ivanovitch Elnikof', but who was actually Ignatei Grinevitsky, came close enough before throwing a second bomb that he was killed along with his victim. An early suicide bomber, one could say. A valuable feature of Footman's book is a biographical appendix on 55 Narodnaya Volya activists. Thirteen were executed, fourteen died in prison, fourteen more survived imprisonment, eight escaped abroad, four committed suicide during or after their *attentats* and two went to work for the secret police.

(1897), Empress Elizabeth of Austria (1898), King Umberto I of Italy (1900, planned in Paterson, New Jersey), US President McKinley (1901), King Alexander of Serbia and his wife (1903), Russian Interior Minister Count Wenzel von Plehve (1904), Grand Duke Sergei of Russia (1905), King Carlos of Portugal and his son Luiz (1908), Prince Ito of Japan (1909), Russian Prime Minister Stolypin (1911), King George of Greece (1913), and of course Archduke Franz Ferdinand and his wife in 1914. Every major state except Germany and Britain.[27] Almost all the assassins were caught and promptly executed.

The storms of Russia were to have profound effects across Europe. They can be symbolically represented in one generation by Bakunin, who died in 1876, and, in the second, by Prince Pyotr Kropotkin, who escaped from Tsarist prison to western Europe that same year. The word anarchist in its technical-political sense was coined in 1877, and spread rapidly and widely, though it was also obvious that there were several competing and cross-pollinating currents of thought about its aims and methods.[28] Anarchism's emphasis on personal liberty and autonomy, its typical suspicion of hierarchical ('bureaucratic') organization, and its penchant for

---

[27] In fact there was at least one abortive plot to kill Kaiser Wilhelm I in 1878, 'uncovered' after an explosion at police headquarters in Frankfurt. Its purported 'anarchist' leader, August Reinsdorf, was quickly executed, while police chief Rumpf was assassinated shortly afterward: a murky affair, in which the manipulative hand of Rumpf is quite probable. In the years 1883 to 1885, there were bomb plots in London against the Tower, Victoria Station and the House of Commons. See Núñez Florencio, *El Terrorismo*, p. 18. These 'events' were quickly reflected in Henry James's *Princess Casamassima* (1886), and much later in Conrad's *The Secret Agent* (1907) and *Under Western Eyes* (1911). Mention should also be made of the May 1882 Fenian assassination of Lord Cavendish, the new Chief Secretary for Ireland, and his undersecretary, though their status was well below of that of the figures mentioned above, and though the Fenians, like the nationalists who killed Franz Ferdinand, were far from being anarchists.

[28] Jean Maitron offers some interesting data in this regard. The single most important theoretical anarchist publication was Jean Grave's *Le Révolté*, first published in safe Geneva in February 1879 with a print run that rose from 1,300 to 2,000 before Grave felt it was possible to relocate it to Paris as *La Révolte* in 1885. By 1894, when it was smashed by the state in the wake of Carnot's assassination, it had a 7,000 print run, with subscribers in France, Algeria, the US, the UK, Switzerland, Belgium, Spain, Holland, Romania, Uruguay, India, Egypt, Guatemala, Brazil, Chile and Argentina. No Russian. Its 'apache' opposite number, Emile Pouget's satirical *Le Père Peignard* ('*Bons bougres, lisez tous les dimanches*') had a comparable 'Atlantic' stretch. See Maitron, *Le Mouvement anarchiste en France*, vol. 1 : *Dès origines à 1914*, Paris 1975, pp. 141–46.

vitriolic rhetoric, made its appeal especially great under political conditions of severe repression by rightwing regimes. Such regimes found
it much easier to smash large trade unions and political parties than
to keep track of and destroy hundreds of self-generated autonomous
groupuscules. Anarchist theory was less contemptuous of peasants and
rural labour than mainstream Marxism was then inclined to be. One
could argue that it was also more viscerally anticlerical. Probably these
conditions help to explain why revolutionary anarchism spread most visibly in still heavily peasant, 'Catholic' post-Commune France, Restoration
Spain, post-unification Italy, Cuba—and even Gilded Age immigrant-
worker America—while prospering much less in Protestant, industrial,
semi-democratic Northern Europe.

In any event, at the end of the bleak 1870s there arose in intellectual
anarchist circles the concept of 'propaganda by the deed', spectacular
violent attacks on reactionary authorities and capitalists, intended both
to intimidate the former, and to encourage cowed workers to re-prepare
themselves for revolution. Historians tend to mark the beginning of this
new phase by the almost comically unsuccessful uprising of April 1877 in
Benevento, northeast of Naples, organized by Errico Malatesta, his rich
friend Carlo Cafiero (who had earlier bankrolled Bakunin from the safe
shores of Lake Maggiore), and Sergei Kravchinsky aka Stepniak, who
had earlier joined the Bosnian uprising against the Turks, and would go
on—as we have seen—to kill the head of the Tsar's secret police. (The
two Italians were acquitted in the cheerful atmosphere created by the
young Umberto I's accession to the throne in 1878. The same ambi-
ence allowed the young anarchist cook Giovanni Passanante to get off
lightly when he narrowly failed to kill the young king with a knife etched
with the words 'Long Live the International Republic'.)[29] Two months
after the Benevento affair, 'comrade' Andrea Costa, a close collaborator
of Malatesta, gave a talk in Geneva theorizing the new 'tactic'. In early
August, Paul Brousse published an article in the radical *Bulletin de la
Fédération Jurassienne* explaining that words on paper were no longer
enough for awakening the *conscience populaire*; the Russians had shown
the need to be just as ruthless as the Tsarist regime. Finally, the gentle
Kropotkin swung into action in the December 25, 1880 edition of *Le
Révolté*, theoretically defining anarchism as 'permanent revolt by means
of the spoken word, writing, the dagger, the gun, and dynamite . . . For

---

[29] Joll, *The Anarchists*, pp. 102–5.

us everything is good which is outside legality'.[30] It remained only for *Le Drapeau Noir* to publish clandestinely on September 2, 1883 a *Manifeste des Nihilistes Français* in which the claim was made that: 'In the three years of the League's existence, several hundred bourgeois families have paid the fatal tribute, devoured by a mysterious sickness that medicine is powerless to define and to exorcise', while revolutionaries were urged to continue the insinuated campaign of mass poisonings (Rizal had just made his first happy trip to Paris a few months before).[31] These were all signs that some anarchists were thinking about a new kind of violence no longer targeted, *à la russe*, against state leaders, but rather indiscriminately against those regarded as class enemies.

Restoration Spain

We can now turn to Rizal's 'third world', that of Spain and its once-vast Empire. (What was left in the 1880s was only Cuba, Puerto Rico, the Philippines, the Marianas and Carolines, Spanish Morocco and the Berlin-acquired, goldless Rio de Oro.) In the nineteenth century, this world was unique in the zigzag of insurrectionary explosions in the metropole and in the colonies. (One will not find anything remotely comparable till after World War II. For France the fuse was laid by Ho Chi Minh's political and Vo Nguyen Giap's military victory at Dien Bien Phu, and set alight by Algeria's FLN revolt—leading to the collapse of the Fourth Republic, De Gaulle's return to power, and the OAS's retaliatory terrorism. For Portugal: military failures in Angola, Mozambique and Guinea-Bissau led to the bloodless coup against Salazarist autocracy in Lisbon in April 1974.) It is worthwhile to consider briefly the main features of this interactive zigzagging, for it was a pattern of which José Rizal was well informed, and by which his thinking was shaped.

In 1808, the odious future Ferdinand VII had organized a military revolt in Aranjuez which accomplished its main aim, the forced abdication of his father Carlos IV. But Napoleon, at the height of his power, took this opportunity to send troops into Spain (occupying Madrid), on the pretext

---

[30] 'la révolte permanente par la parole, par l'écrit, par le poignard, le fusil, la dynamite . . . Tout est bon pour nous qui n'est pas la légalité'. Maitron, *Le Mouvement*, pp. 77–78.
[31] 'Depuis trois ans que la ligue existe, plusieurs centaines de familles bourgeoises ont payé le fatal tribut, dévorées par un mal mystérieux que la médecine est impuissante á définir et á conjurer'. Maitron, *Le Mouvement*, p. 206.

of a major intervention in Portugal. Fernando VII, who had rushed to Bayonne to negotiate legitimization of his succession with the Secretary of the World-Spirit, was immediately imprisoned. Joseph Bonaparte was then put on the Spanish throne. Resistance and rebellion broke out almost simultaneously in Andalusia and in Hidalgo's Mexico. In 1810, a liberal-dominated Cortes met in Cádiz, which produced in 1812 Spain's first constitutional order. The colonies, including the Philippines, were given legislative representation.[32] Napoleon's defeat brought Fernando back to power in Madrid with the full support of the Holy Alliance. In 1814, he refused to recognize the Constitution, inaugurated a new reactionary absolutism and, in spite of a ruined economy, attempted to arrest the American revolutions for whom nationalism and in-Spain-repressed liberalism were the two main principles. Fernando failed completely in continental Spanish America, but held the loyalty of slave-owning peninsulars and creoles in the Spanish Caribbean—out of Bolívar's charismatic orbit, and petrified by the successful slave revolution in Haiti. And the Philippines? The 'Sarrat' revolt of 1815 in the Ilokano-populated northwest corner of Luzon was quickly and violently repressed. In 1820, however, a military revolt in Andalusia, headed by the mayor of Cádiz, forced Fernando briefly to accept a liberal constitutional order. But Castlereagh's London, Metternich's Vienna, Alexander I's Petersburg, and Ferdinand's kinsman in Paris would have none of this. A French military expedition restored autocracy in 1823, the mayor of Cádiz was hanged, drawn and quartered, and hundreds of liberals and republicans were executed, brutally imprisoned or forced to flee for their lives. That same year, and in response to these events in the metropole, occurred the creole-led 'Novales Mutiny' in the colonial military which came within an ace of seizing Manila, and would have done so had it not been betrayed from within.[33]

One can easily detect a comparable conjuncture in the years 1868–74. Isabella's regime was overthrown in September 1868 by a military-civil

---

[32] The Philippines kept this representation in all subsequent 'constitutional moments', until its rights were abolished—well after the collapse of the South American Empire—in 1837. Rizal told his friend Blumentritt that his maternal grandfather had in fact sat as a Philippine representative in this metropolitan legislature. See letter of November 8, 1888, from London, in *Rizal-Blumentritt Correspondence*, vol. 1, third unnumbered page after p. 268.

[33] D. G. E. Hall. *A History of South-East Asia* [3rd ed.], London and New York 1968, p. 721. For details on these commotions, typically organized by creoles, see Sarkisyanz, *Rizal*, pp. 76–79.

coup in which General Prim y Prats, the Machiavellian liberal politician Práxedes Sagasta, and the conspiracy-minded radical republican Ruiz Zorilla were key players. We have already seen the consequences of this 'explosion' in Cuba and the Philippines. But in Spain itself the next six years were ones of extraordinary political turbulence. Prim y Prats's assassination at the end of 1870 doomed the monarchy of Amadeo of Savoy, which led to the proclamation of a Spanish Republic on February 11, 1873. The new regime lasted in reality only eleven months—during which time it experienced four Swiss-style rotating presidents—till the generals moved in (guided behind the scenes by the sly Andalusian conservative politician Antonio Cánovas del Castillo), dissolving the Cortes in January 1874, and restoring the Bourbon monarchy in the person of Alfonso XII at the end of that year. Among the key reasons for this *démarche* was, as one might have surmised, the imminent threat posed by Céspedes's Cuban revolt to the integrity of what was left of the old Spanish empire. Meantime, however, there was an extraordinary Durkheimian effervescence in the Spanish public sphere. Republicans were briefly legal for the first time in living memory. Bakuninian and Marxian radicalism gained their first political footholds, and in the widely popular 'cantonalist' political movement of 1873 for radical decentralization of the polity, many young anarchists and other radicals got their first experience of open, mass politics. (Nor was this the end of the chain of zigzags, as we shall see. Martí's insurrection in Cuba at the beginning of 1895, which also had its antecedents in anarchist Barcelona, encouraged Andrés Bonifacio's revolt in the Philippines in August 1896, helped sentence Rizal to death four months later, and in 1897 led to Cánovas's assassination by a young Italian anarchist.)

With this background we can now consider Restoration Spain as Rizal encountered it at the beginning of the 1880s. Its dominant politician, Cánovas, liked to say that he was a great admirer of British parliamentary government, and proceeded to set up, with the help of Sagasta, a peculiar parody of the Gladstone–Disraeli duumvirate. Schumacher has pithily described a corrupt, cacique-ridden regime which lasted essentially till the end of the century:

> [T]he two leaders permitted the entire system to be vitiated through managed elections . . . As more serious crises came to be resolved, each would yield power to the other and the successor government would *then* proceed to manage an election in which a respectable minority of candidates would

be elected with a scattering of outstanding republicans and Carlists to give verisimilitude to the Cortes.'[34]

The Spanish Disraeli ruled from 1875–81, 1883–85, 1890–92, and 1895–97, while 'Gladstone' filled the spaces in between. The worst domestic and colonial repressions typically occurred under Cánovas, while timid reforms were usually accomplished under Sagasta.

Friar power

For what follows next, it is crucial to understand Cánovas's policies toward the generally reactionary Spanish Church. In 1836, First Minister Juan Mendizábal had decreed and carried out the expropriation of all the property of the religious Orders in Spain; and during Glorious 1868, Antonio Ortiz, Minister of Gracia y Justicia, had abolished the Orders themselves—in metropolitan Spain. Mendizábal was no Thomas Cromwell: the Orders were 'compensated' by being put on the state's payroll. The clerical properties were put up for auction and, especially in rich rural Andalusia, were snapped up by members of the nobility, high civilian and military officials, and wealthy bourgeois, many of them absentee. Relatively mild Church exploitation was succeeded by ruthless agribusiness methods; hundreds of thousands of peasants lost access to land, and swelled the numbers of paupers, half-starved day-labourers, and the 'bandits' for which the region became famous after 1840. Andalusian Cánovas made no attempt to roll back what Mendizábal had decreed, though he sought and secured strong Church backing against the rising tide of liberalism, masonry, republicanism, socialism and anarchism.[35] (It was he who in 1884 sent the police into Central University at the call of the bishops.) Nor did he restore the independent position of the Orders, who, after all, were directly responsible to Rome not to himself. But there was one striking exception to all these changes—and that was the colonial Philippines.

It had begun centuries earlier, in the time of Felipe II. The conscience of the ageing monarch had been sufficiently stung by the revelations of de las Casas and others of the inhuman depredations of the conquistadors in the Americas that he decided to entrust his last major imperial acquisition

---

[34] Schumacher, *Propaganda Movement*, pp. 21–22. My italics.
[35] On Mendizábal and Ortiz, see Schumacher, *Propaganda Movement*, p. 134, fn. 16. More generally on the consequences of the confiscation of Order properties, especially in Andalusia, see Bécarud and Lapouge, *Anarchistes*, pp. 14–20.

largely to the Orders, who indeed managed the relatively peaceful conversion of the bulk of the local population. The remote Philippines had no 'lay' attractions comparable to Potosí, and so the Orders largely ran the colony, especially outside Manila. In the course of time, especially the Dominicans and Augustinians acquired vast properties both in Manila real-estate and in *hacienda* agriculture. Furthermore, from the start the Orders had insisted on carrying out conversion via the dozens of native languages (only then would conversions be deep and sincere) which they assiduously attempted to learn. This monopoly on linguistic access to the natives gave them enormous power which no secular group shared; fully aware of this, the friars persistently opposed the spread of the Spanish language. Even in Rizal's time, it has been estimated that only about 3 per cent of the population of the archipelago had any command of the metropolitan language, something unique in the Spanish empire (with the partial exception of ex-Jesuit Paraguay). In the nineteenth century the Spanish political class understood this situation very well, and perhaps rightly reckoned that, without the Orders, Spanish rule in the Philippines would collapse. Hence the only Order-controlled seminaries tolerated in Spain after Ortiz's time were there simply to provide new young friars for the Philippines. At the same time many friars, traumatized by their 'defenestration' in Spain, headed off for safety and power on the other side of the world. Thus, in the Cánovas era, friar power was as peculiar to the Philippines as slavery was to Cuba. But (thanks to Sagasta) slavery was finally abolished in 1886, while in Manila (no thanks to Sagasta) friar power was not seriously undermined till the collapse of the whole system in 1898. From another angle, one can see that Filipino anticolonial activists were inevitably faced with a hard choice which was not open to Cubans and Puerto Ricans: to reject Spanish or spread it. We shall see later on how this question shaped the narrative of *El Filibusterismo*.

Internationale

When an alarmed Captain-General Izquierdo had suspected the machinations of the International behind the extraordinary strike of the autumn of 1872, what made the idea plausible to him? After Isabella fled Madrid in September 1868, Bakunin was much quicker off the mark than Marx. He immediately sent his Italian friend, ex-Mazzinist, ex-Garibaldist Giuseppe Fanelli, to Barcelona and Madrid to inform and organize the 'most advanced' local radical activists. In spite of the fact that Fanelli knew no Spanish, he had an instant and powerful impact. The Centro

Federal de las Sociedades Obreras was formed early the following year, and sent two Bakuninist delegates to swell the Russian's majority at the Basle Congress of the International in September.[36] Early in 1870 the Federación Regional Española, the Spanish section of the International, was publishing *La Solidaridad,* and a little later held its first and only Congress in early-industrial Barcelona.[37]

Meantime, Marx's Cuban son-in-law, Paul Lafargue, who had been with the Commune in Paris, but then moved to Bordeaux to widen support for the Parisian insurrectionaries, finally fled across the Pyrenees with his family (his newborn baby died en route).[38] Once settled in Madrid in June 1871, under the alias Pablo Fargas, he followed Marx's instructions to combat the influence of the Bakuninists. But it was pretty late in the day. In December, the Cortes banned the International. During the year or so he was in Spain, he had no luck in Bakuninist Barcelona, but did help start a Marxist group in Madrid. Lafargue was the only pro-Marx 'Spanish' delegate at the disastrous fifth Congress of the International in The Hague in 1872. Not till 1879 was a semi-clandestine Marxist Socialist Party formed and it did not come out of the closet till the rule of Sagasta in the early 1880s. Its organ, *El Obrero,* first appeared in 1882.[39] Many more years would pass before it became a central player in the politics of the Spanish Left. There is no special reason to think that Rizal ever heard of it while a student in Madrid.

---

[36] The International's first two congresses, held in peaceable Switzerland in 1866 and 1867, had gone ahead quietly enough with Marx in the central position. But Bakunin's influence was already strongly felt at the third congress in Brussels in 1868, and Bakuninists were a majority at the fourth congress in Basle. The fifth congress was supposed to assemble in Paris, but Sedan made this impossible. By the time it was finally held in 1872, in The Hague, it was hopelessly divided. In the year of Bakunin's death it was dissolved, though Bakuninist congresses continued to be held till 1877. See the succinct account in Maitron, *Le Mouvement,* pp. 42–51.

[37] George Esenwein, *Anarchist Ideology and the Working Class Movement in Spain, 1868–1898,* Berkeley 1989, pp. 14–18; Bécarud and Lapouge, *Anarchistes,* pp. 27–29.

[38] How did a Cuban manage so fine a French name? His grandparents on both sides had been 'French Haitians', and had moved to Cuba to escape Toussaint's revolution. One grandfather (Lafargue) was a small slave-owning planter and the other (Abraham Armagnac) a Jewish merchant. One grandmother was a Haitian mulatta, and the other a Jamaican Caribe. Both Paul and his parents were born in Santiago de Cuba. The family moved back to the grandfather's native Bordeaux in 1851, escaping this time from Cuban rebellion and Spanish repression. Paul carried a Spanish passport, and was bilingual in French and Spanish.

[39] Bécarud and Lapouge, *Anarchistes,* pp. 29–34; David Ortiz, Jr., *Paper Liberals, Press and Politics in Restoration Spain,* Westport, CT 2000, p. 58.

But he was certainly well aware of what developed next, and we shall find traces of this in *El Filibusterismo*. Cánovas's six-year regime of repression was replaced by the milder, more permissive Sagasta in 1881, very soon after the assassination of Alexander II, and after a meeting in London of various anarchists had moved to confirm the necessity of violent 'propaganda by the deed'. The change of government in Spain allowed the FRE top leadership, mostly Catalan, to believe the way was now open for wider, and legal, organizing of the working class, and in September it replaced the FRE by the FTRE (Federación de Trabajadores de la Región Española). Since this policy diverged from the radical resolutions approved in London, they did what they could to keep these decisions under wraps. But the news leaked out anyway. In spite of a spectacular increase in its affiliated membership—58,000 people in one year—tension grew quickly between the 'legalists' in industrial Barcelona and the radicals with their base in rural Andalusia. At the 1882 Congress in Seville, most of the Andalusians broke away to form a group they called The Disinherited (Los Desheredados). 1883 was a difficult year in any case. A world-wide depression had set in, with especially severe consequences in Andalusia, where hunger and immiseration grew rapidly. Furthermore, Cánovas returned to power. A new wave of rural arson and robbery spread all over the Prime Minister's home region, causing real panic in many places.[40] The police arrested and tortured hundreds of people, anarchists, peasants and bandits, claiming shortly thereafter to have uncovered a vast secret insurrectionary conspiracy called La Mano Negra [Black Hand].[41] Far from offering its support, the FTRE, hoping to avoid repression, firmly disassociated itself from what it termed criminal activities. This stance did not help, and the organization declined steadily till its dissolution in 1888.[42] We shall see that the spectre of La Mano Negra and the Andalusian panic are reflected in the latter half of *El Filibusterismo*.

---

[40] According to Bécarud and Lapouge, *Anarchistes*, p. 36, an earlier such wave had occurred in 1878–80.

[41] Ramón Sempau observed that now '*se renovaron prácticas olvidadas*'—'forgotten practices [i.e. of the Inquisition era] were renewed'. *Los Victimarios*, p. 275. Two famous Spanish novels, published a quarter of a century later under a liberalized regime, afford fine evocations of the 'undergrounds' of Barcelona and Andalusia in this period: Pío Baroja's *Aurora Roja* [Red Dawn] and Vicente Blasco Ibáñez's *La Bodega* [The Cellar], both originally published in Madrid in 1905.

[42] See the succinct account of these developments in Núñez Florencio, *El Terrorismo*, pp. 38–42.

Rizal's homecoming

Sagasta returned to power in 1885, and held it until 1890. It was this government that finally abolished slavery in Cuba, enacted a rather liberal law on associations which allowed radicals to start organizing legally once again, and substantially expanded press freedom. It even made some serious attempts at reforms in the Philippines. In 1887 the Spanish Penal Code was extended to the archipelago, followed in 1889 by a similar extension of the Spanish Code of Commerce, the law on administrative litigation, and the Civil Code, except with regard to marriage (the Church in the Philippines bitterly insisted on this). But it was exactly in July 1885 that Rizal left Spain more or less for good, proceeding to France and Germany, and busying himself with further medical studies and with the completion of his first novel. When it was published in the spring of 1887, he decided the time had come to return to the Philippines. He went to Austria to meet for the first and last time his favourite correspondent Blumentritt, toured Switzerland, visited Rome, and sailed for Southeast Asia from Marseilles, arriving home on August 5. (But he left again for Europe only six months later.)

On coming to power for the second time, Sagasta had appointed a new, relatively moderate Captain-General in the Philippines, Lt. Gen. Emilio Terrero y Perinat, who in turn relied heavily on two capable anticlerical subordinates, both of them Masons: the civil governor of Manila, José Centeno García, a mining engineer with republican sympathies, and an unusual twenty years of experience in the Philippines, and the director-general of civil administration, Benigno Quiroga López Ballesteros, a younger man who had once been a liberal deputy in the Cortes. (Centeno would appear, unnamed but honored, in *El Filibusterismo*.) The two men vigorously enforced laws which took municipal justice away from the mayors and gave them to new justices of the peace, and likewise reassigned the provincial governors' judicial powers to judges of the first instance. The intended effect of both measures was to cut back the power of the friars, who had traditionally held undisputed sway over local government via local executives.[43]

News of *Noli Me Tangere* (and a few copies) had preceded Rizal's return home, and he found himself a famous, or infamous man. The Orders

---

[43] Compare Guerrero, *First Filipino*, pp. 178–80, with Schumacher, *Propaganda Movement*, pp. 109–14.

and the Archbishop of Manila demanded that the book be prohibited as heretical, subversive and slanderous, and the author suitably punished. But, perhaps to his own surprise, Rizal was summoned to a tête-à-tête with Terrero himself, who said he wanted to read the novel, and asked for a copy. We do not know what the Captain-General thought of it, but the novel was not banned under his rule.[44] After a few days in Manila, Rizal returned home to Calamba to be with his family, and open a medical practice. Then his many enemies went to work. In a letter to Blumentritt of September 5, 1887 he wrote: 'I get threats every day . . . My father never lets me go for a walk alone, or dine with another family. The Old Man is terrified and trembles. People take me for a German spy or agent; they say I am an agent of Bismarck, a Protestant, a Freemason, a sorcerer, a half-damned soul, etc. So I stay at home.'[45]

Worse was to follow. As noted earlier, Rizal's family wealth rested on the extensive lands it leased from the local Dominican *hacienda*. From the time of the 1883–86 depression the friars had started raising rents steeply, even as world sugar prices collapsed. Furthermore they appropriated other lands to which, the townspeople felt, they had no just claim. About the time that Rizal returned, various tenants, including relatives of Rizal, stopped paying rent, and appealed to Manila to intervene on their behalf. Suspecting that the Dominicans were cheating on their taxes, Terrero sent a commission to investigate, but then did nothing. At this point the friars went on the attack by getting court orders for evictions. Rizal's family was deliberately chosen as the main target. Both sides went up the legal hierarchy over the next four years, even to the Supreme Court in Spain, but unsurprisingly the Dominicans prevailed.

---

[44] Guerrero, *First Filipino*, p. 180.
[45] 'man droht mich jeden Tag . . . Mein Vater lässt mich nie allein spazieren, noch bei einer anderen Familie essen; der Alte fürchtet und zittert. Man hält mich für einen deutschen Espion oder Agent; man sagt ich sei Bismarck Agent, Protestant, Freimason, Zauberer, Halbverdammte Seele u.s.w. Darum bleibe ich zu Hause.' *Rizal-Blumentritt Correspondence*, Vol. 1, fifth unnumbered page following p. 133. Bismarck was an ogre for clerical circles because of his decade-long Kulturkampf of the 1870s, intended to coerce German Catholics into giving their first loyalty to the Reich. (It was partly his reaction to the promulgation of Papal Infallibility.) But there was also wider fear of his designs on Spanish Oceania. It seems that in 1885 the Reichskanzler had announced that the imperial navy would ensure the safety of German entrepreneurs in the Carolines. Spanish troops were sent off hurriedly to put down resistance there to the full imposition of Madrid's sovereignty. In *El Filibusterismo*, the nice student Isagani expresses his strong sympathy with the *insulares*. (Ch. xxiv, 'Sueños [Dreams]').

In the meantime members of Rizal's family were evicted from their homes, and other recalcitrant townspeople were soon treated the same way. By then Rizal himself had been advised by everyone to leave the country, since he was suspected of masterminding the resistance.

In early 1888 Terrero's term was up, and the Sagasta government, under heavy political pressure from conservatives at home and in the colony, made the fateful decision to appoint in his stead General Valeriano Weyler, a man with a reputation for 'severity' from Havana—and later, in the middle 1890s, to become world-notorious as the 'Butcher of Cuba'.[46] Terrero's liberal advisers were quickly dismissed or transferred. In 1891 Weyler would be the man who finally 'solved' the problem of tenant recalcitrance in Calamba by sending in a detachment of artillerymen to burn several houses to the ground, and forcibly clear lots 'illegally' occupied. In *El Filibusterismo* Weyler appears, unnamed, as the central target of Simoun's jewelled-pomegranate bomb. It is not surprising then that Rizal delayed his final return to the Philippines until after the general's term was over.

The making of a filibustero

Rizal's decision to live in London on his return to Europe was spurred by the priceless research collection of the British Museum. From newspapers and journals he was perfectly aware of the rising tide of nationalism within the dynastic empires of Europe, to say nothing of Cuba, the

---

[46] Weyler (b. 1838) spent almost all of the first ten years (1863–73) of his career in the Caribbean. It will be recalled that the First Dominican Republic had successfully broken away from Haiti in 1844, but in 1861, at President Pedro Santana's initiative, had been taken back into the Spanish Empire. In 1863 a popular revolt broke out—aided by Haiti—against this 'treason'. Weyler was among the first young officers to be sent from Cuba to crush the insurrection. Pressured by the us, and by military reverses, Madrid was forced two years later to withdraw its troops and recognize the Second Dominican Republic. Weyler made his reputation as an outstanding officer (he was the youngest man of his time to achieve general rank) by his successes against the Céspedes revolt in Cuba. He earned the soubriquet *el sanguinario* by his leadership of ruthless 'hunter' (*cazadores*) units of lumpen or criminal volunteers. Even a fervent admirer concedes that he killed more prisoners than any other Spanish officer. On his return to Madrid, he was assigned the task of smashing the Carlist forces in Valencia, and accomplished it successfully—without Cuban-style methods. See the hilarious *franquista* hagiography by General Hilario Martín Jiménez, *Valeriano Weyler, De Su Vida y Personalidad, 1838–1930*, Santa Cruz de Tenerife 1998, chs. 2–6, and especially on dead prisoners p. 247.

Ottoman Empire, and the East. Central to all these nationalisms' articulation were the efforts of folklorists, historians, lexicographers, poets, novelists and musicians to resurrect glorious pasts behind humiliating presents and, especially through replacing imperial languages by local vernaculars, to build and consolidate national identities. He had never forgotten the early shock of being misrecognized as a Chinese, Japanese or *americano*, and of realizing that his country was basically unknown in Europe. Furthermore, he was aware that unlike, for example, Malaya, Burma, India, Ceylon, Cambodia and Vietnam, no precolonial written records in his country had survived European conquest. Such Philippine history as existed was the product of members of the Orders or, later, of racist Spanish conservatives. His concern in this regard was also rivalrously stimulated by the somewhat older Isabelo de los Reyes, whose landmark *El Folk-Lore Filipino* had surprisingly won a prize at the Madrid Exposition of 1887.[47] In the British Museum he found what he was looking for, a very rare copy of *Sucesos de las Islas Filipinas* of Dr Antonio de Morga, published in Mexico in 1609. (Morga had arrived in the Philippines in 1595 at the age of thirty-four, to take the positions of Justice of the Audiencia in Manila, and lieutenant-governor. He was a rarity in his time, an austerely honest colonial official whose realistic outlook was not clouded by clerical prejudices.) After laboriously copying out this book by hand, Rizal decided to get it republished with extensive annotations and commentaries of his own, most of which were designed, by comparison with clerical chronicles, to show the reliability of Morga's generally favourable account of native society—its level of civilization, its peaceful productivity and its commercial relations with China, Japan and parts of Southeast Asia. He managed to publish the book with Garnier in Paris, officially in 1890, but in fact late in 1889.[48]

Though Rizal's Morga was not widely read then, or later, it clearly represents a turning point in his own political trajectory. He was becoming a *filibustero*, a patriot determined one way or the other on his country's full independence. (As we shall see, *El Filibusterismo* shows this new stance extremely clearly.) One consequence—given the prestige he

---

[47] On this fascinating and pioneering, work, see my 'The Rooster's Egg', NLR 2, March–April 2000. We shall see a lot of Isabelo later on, in Part III.
[48] In his *First Filipino*, Guerrero has a lengthy and interesting discussion both of Morga's original and of Rizal's annotations (pp. 205–23). It has to be said that some of Rizal's closest friends, such as Blumentritt and the painter Juan Luna, privately suggested to him that his patriotism had led him into exaggerations. De los Reyes was politely critical on the same grounds in public.

had won among Filipinos by *Noli Me Tangere* and a spate of powerfully written articles published in various republican newspapers in Spain— was a growing schism within the overseas Filipino community in the metropole. Even during his student days in Spain, Rizal had frequently criticized his fellow-countrymen there for frivolity, womanizing, idleness, gossip-mongering, drunkenness and the like. Although he retained a number of close friends there, his years away in Northern Europe had deepened his irritation and sense of alienation.

Yet there was an interesting moment of partial reconvergence. At the end of 1888 a group of the more serious Filipinos there decided to take advantage of Sagasta's 1887 law liberalizing political space to form themselves into an energetic new political organization and to publish their own journal, to be called *La Solidaridad*. Barcelona's atmosphere was a significant element in these decisions. The influential anarchist journal *La Acracia* had already started publication in Barcelona, at the same time that in Madrid Pablo Iglesias's (Marxist) Socialist Party put out *El Socialista*. In 1887, Barcelona's anarchists finally had their own successful daily, *El Productor*.[49] Republican and anarchist organizations were proliferating along with many others. The Filipino initiatives were focused by the arrival in January 1889 of Marcelo del Pilar, the most capable Filipino politician of his generation. Del Pilar's elder brother, a native priest, had been arrested and deported to the Marianas in Izquierdo's repression of 1872, and Marcelo was an agile anti-friar and nationalist organizer

[49] See Ortiz, *Paper Liberals*, pp. 57–60. Ortiz comments that these productions, as well as the later *La Revista Blanca*, showed that the lively anarchist press 'surpassed the socialist press in intellectual rigour, circulation, and longevity'. He also points out the massive new popularity of reading clubs where—given the widespread illiteracy of Barcelona's working class—'readers' (*lectores*) read out loud from the press. It is quite remarkable that two *El Productors* appeared in the same year, one in Barcelona, and the other in Havana under the chief editorship of the energetic Catalan anarchist Enrique Roig y San Martín, whose Circulo de Trabajadores also issued a bimonthly Bakuninist magazine called *Hijos del Mundo*. I owe this information to an unpublished paper 'Leaves of Change: Cuban Tobacco Workers and the Struggle against Slavery and Spanish Imperial Rule, 1880s–1890s', by Evan Daniel (2003), at pp. 23–24. My thanks to Robin Blackburn (and Evan Daniel) for allowing me to read it. Daniel says that the Havana *El Productor* regularly reprinted articles from Barcelona's *La Acracia* (as well as translations from *Le Révolté* and other non-Spanish anarchist periodicals), but does not mention its Barcelona twin, which is puzzling. Daniel also emphasizes the enormous importance of *lectores* for the many illiterate tobacco-workers. All of this offers a striking contrast between Havana and Manila in this period: a vigorous and legal anarchist press could flourish in Cuba, while nothing remotely comparable would ever have been tolerated in the Philippines.

under the permissive rule of Terrero, Centeno and Quiroga. But after Weyler's arrival he knew he was a marked man, and so escaped to Spain. He immediately took over leadership of the Filipino activists and their new journal, eventually moving it to Madrid to be closer to the centre of state power. From then on, till his miserable, poverty-stricken death in Barcelona in July 1896, he never left Spain.

While Del Pilar's goal was certainly eventual Philippine independence, and while he actively promoted close ties with Manila and encouraged organizing there, he was convinced that the necessary first major steps had to be taken in Spain itself. 'Liberal' cabinets, along with liberal and republican members of the Cortes, had to be lobbied by every means available to create the institutional spaces in which independence could eventually be achieved—while concealing this ultimate goal as much as possible. The tactical steps that had to be taken were basically to catch up with Cuba, via a programme of assimilation. Cuba had representation in the Cortes but the Philippines, as we have seen, had lost this right in 1837. After the abolition of slavery in 1886, Cuba had basically the same legal system as Spain. The Caribbean colony was Spanish-speaking, its educational system was basically secular and state-provided, and the Church's political power was relatively low. Though Del Pilar was an accomplished writer in Tagalog (more so than Rizal, in fact), and though he privately discussed language-policy in a future independent Philippines, he was sure that at this stage only assimilation and hispanicization would create the political atmosphere in which Madrid would permit the Philippines to assume Cuba's political status. Pushing through a serious state-sponsored Spanish-language educational system in the Philippines would also have the effect of destroying the foundations of the Orders' peculiar dominance in his country.[50]

---

[50] Schumacher's *Propaganda Movement* provides an astute and generally sympathetic account of Del Pilar's life, ideas, goals, and political activities. The paragraph above is a wholly inadequate micro-version of his argument. This may be the place to say something brief about Cuban–Filipino contacts in Spain, such as they were. A good many Filipinos who became Masons in the metropole joined lodges largely composed of Cubans, probably because the Cubans were more friendly and welcoming than the Spaniards. Rafael Labra, a senior creole Cuban member of the republican group in the Cortes (sitting for Puerto Rico and Asturias), with a strong autonomist programme, was not only intellectually influential through his voluminous writings on colonial questions, but also regularly attended and spoke at 'political banquets' organized by Filipino activists. He had earlier headed the first abolitionist movement in Spain—in the 1860s! (Thomas, *Cuba*, p. 240.) Beyond this, the ties

Though utterly different in temperament and talent, Rizal and Del Pilar respected one another, and for a time Rizal wrote energetically for the new journal. But fairly soon, partly as the result of intrigues and jealousies among the lesser activists, they grew apart. After February 1891 Rizal announced that he would write no more for *La Solidaridad*, though he would always give it his moral support. The novelist was increasingly certain that the whole assimilationist campaign was futile. Politically, Cuban representation in the Cortes was meaningless under the corrupt Cánovas–Sagasta electoral system. It had not stopped Spain from continued merciless exploitation of Cuban production through manipulated tariffs, monopolies and subjection to Basque and Catalan business interests. So dissatisfied with 'assimilation' was Cuba, in fact, that, exactly as Madrid feared, the demand was now for autonomy—home rule in effect, heading in the direction of that independence which most of Spanish America had achieved more than half a century earlier. Besides, Rizal believed, there was no chance whatever, at the end of the nineteenth century, of turning millions of Filipinos into assimilated Spanish-speakers. Sagasta's sending the brutal Weyler to Manila in 1888, and his own replacement by Cánovas in 1890, further deepened Rizal's conviction that nothing could be successfully achieved in Spain. The work of emancipation would have to be done back home.

It was in this frame of mind that he moved to Belgium where the cost of living better fitted his meagre resources, and where printing was said to be cheaper than in the surrounding big states. There he worked on *El Filibusterismo*, seeing it frantically through press in August 1891, after which he immediately headed home. If *Noli Me Tangere* was targeted at multiple audiences in Europe and the Philippines, *El Filibusterismo* was meant only for the latter. He sent a few copies to personal friends in Spain and elsewhere, but the rest of the entire edition was shipped to Hong Kong, where he intended to settle till Weyler's term was over. To his trusted older friend Basa, one of the deported victims of Izquierdo twenty years earlier who had settled in Hong Kong and become a successful businessman (and agile smuggler), he wrote an important letter from Ghent on July 9 entrusting the books to him, and urging complete

seem to have been rather minimal. Cuba's political status was far in advance of that of the Philippines, its representatives in Spain were more likely to be peninsulars and creoles (rather than *mestizos* or 'natives'), and the problems of the two colonies were very different. I know of no Cuban who ever visited the Spanish Philippines, and no more than one or two Filipinos who, in the late colonial period, had seen Cuba at first hand.

secrecy in the face of clerical espionage which also stretched into the British colony. The letter is very bitter about his own extreme poverty, and the endless broken promises of financial help from rich members of the Filipino community in Spain:

> I am tired of trusting in our fellow countrymen; they all seem to have joined hands to embitter my life ⸱ . . Ah! I tell you [frankly], that if it were not for you, if it were not that I believe that there are still [some] genuinely good Filipinos, I would readily send fellow countrymen and all to the devil! What do they take me for? Exactly at the moment when one needs to keep one's spirit tranquil and one's imagination free, they come at one with intrigues and petty meannesses![51]

A missing library?

After this too-extended historical background, we can now reconsider some of the puzzles that face the reader of Rizal's second novel, especially its apparently proleptic aspects. But before doing so, one serious investigative difficulty needs brief discussion. If one considers what books Rizal had in his library in the Philippines, what is plain is that there are no volumes by political thinkers after the time of Voltaire, Rousseau and Herder, unless we include Herbert Spencer. Rizal's vast published correspondence shows the same pattern. No mention of Constant, Tocqueville, Comte, Saint-Simon, Fourier, Bentham, Mill, Marx, Bakunin, Kropotkin, Hegel or Fichte—only one-sentence casual allusions to Proudhon and Tolstoy. It is true that Rizal was a novelist, poet and moralist more than a political analyst, but it is hard to believe that over the almost ten years he spent in Madrid, Paris, London and Berlin, he managed to avoid or ignore all these influential thinkers. There is, so far, only one direct clue—a letter written to him in Brussels by his close friend in Paris, Juan Luna. In this letter, the painter reported that he had been reading with great interest a book by the Belgian polymath and renowned bimetallic political economist Emile de Laveleye (1822–92):

> I have been reading *Le Socialisme contemporain* by E. de Laveleye, which is a compilation of the theories of Karl Marx, Lassalle, etc., Catholic

---

51 'Estoy cansado ya de creer en nuestros paisanos; todos parece que se han unído por amargarme la vida . . . Ah! Le digo a V., que si no fuera por V., si no fuera porque creo que hay todavía verdaderos buenos filipinos, me dan ganas de enviar al diablo paisanos y todo! Por quién me han tomado? Precisamente, cuando uno necesita tener su espíritu tranquilo y su imaginación libre, venirle á uno con engaños y mezquindades!' *Epistolario Rizalino*, vol. 3 (1890–92), ed. Teodoro M. Kalaw, Manila 1935, pp. 200–01.

Paciano Mercado, you are called the entire people of Calamba!'⁵⁶ Ubaldo
and Hidalgo were Rizal's brothers-in-law, while Paciano was his elder
brother. All were severely punished for resisting the Dominicans in
1888–90. And 'San Diego' is calmly unmasked as 'Kalamba'.⁵⁷ Later in the
novel, we learn that Tales joins the bandits, and after his daughter Julí's
suicide to escape Father Camorra's lust, allies himself with Simoun, and
finally becomes Matanglawin ('Hawk-eye'), the uncaught bandit chief
who terrorizes the whole countryside around Manila. Historically, there
seems to have been no figure like Matanglawin in the Philippines of that
time, though there were plenty of small bandits in the hilly country to
the south of the colonial capital. But were there perhaps one or two in
the violent, hungry Andalusia of Rizal's student days?

Transpositions

The main subplot of *El Filibusterismo* is, as mentioned earlier, the ultimately unsuccessful campaign of the students to have the state establish
an academy for (lay) instruction in the Spanish language—the first step
towards the hispanicization of the population. In historical fact, there
was never any such student campaign in Manila, and in any case Weyler
would not have tolerated it for a moment. But the subplot is visibly a
satirical microcosmic version of the tactical assimilation campaign conducted by Del Pilar in Spain from 1889 onward—in which Rizal had lost
all faith. The detailed picture of the students seems completely unlike
the one we can gain from other sources of the high school and college
world Rizal experienced in Manila in the late 1870s, virtually innocent of
politics. Almost to a man, the students in *El Filibusterismo* are depicted
as gossips, opportunists, blowhards, cynics, rich do-nothings, spongers
and cheats. The only one who is painted as goodhearted and patriotic,
the *indio* Isagani, is still a firm, naïve believer in the campaign, and

---

⁵⁶ 'Tranquilizaos, pacíficos vecinos de Kalamba! Ninguno de vosotros se llama
Tales, ninguno de vosotros ha cometido el crímen! Vosotros os llamáis . . . Silvestre
Ubaldo, Manuel Hidalgo, Paciano Mercado, os llamáis todo el pueblo de Kalamba!'
This apostrophe is how Chapter x ends. It is reminiscent of the famous ending to
Dekker's *Max Havelaar*, where the author casts aside his characters and his plot to
launch a hair-raising broadside in his own name at the Dutch colonial regime in the
Indies and its backers in the Netherlands.
⁵⁷ One of Rizal's political hobbies at this time was to insist on spelling Tagalog
words, even when, or perhaps especially when, they derived from Spanish, with
his own orthographic system. One of the provocations involved was to substitute
the aggressively non-Castilian 'k' for 'c' and 'w' for 'ue'. Hence *pwede* for *puede* and,
here, Kalamba for Calamba.

without any serious political ideas. It is thus not easy to avoid the conclusion that almost the entire subplot is simply historical Spain oceanically transferred to an imagined Manila.

But this is by no means all. In the crucial early chapter ('Simoun') in which the reader learns—because Basilio accidentally recognizes him—that Simoun is actually Ibarra, the naïve hero of *Noli Me Tangere*, the question of the campaign is introduced into their conversation. To the reader's probable surprise, the cynical 'nihilist' conspirator Simoun sounds, as it were, a violently Basque or Polish note.[58]

> Ah youth! Always naïve, always dreaming, always running after butterflies and flowers. You unite so that by your efforts you can bind your motherland [*patria*] to Spain with garlands of roses, when in fact you are forging chains harder than a diamond! You ask for equality of rights, and the hispanization of your customs, without understanding that what you ask for is death, the destruction of your nationality [*nacionalidad*], the obliteration of your motherland, and the consecration of tyranny! What will you become in the future? A people [*pueblo*] without character, a nation without liberty; everything in you will be borrowed, even your very defects. You ask for hispanization, and you do not blanch with shame when it is denied you! And even if it be granted to you, what do you want with it? What would you gain? If you are lucky, a country of pronunciamentos, a country of civil wars, a republic of predators and malcontents like some of the republics of South America! . . . Spanish will never be the common language in this country, the people will never speak it, because that language does not have the words to express the ideas in their minds and the sentiments in their hearts. Each people has its own, as it has its own way of feeling. What will you gain from Spanish, the few of you who speak it? Kill your originality, subordinate your thoughts to other minds, and instead of making yourselves free, turn yourselves into veritable slaves! Nine out of ten of you who presume yourselves *ilustrados* are renegades to your country. Those who speak Spanish forget their own tongue, which they no longer write or understand. How many have I seen who pretend not to know a single word of it! Luckily you have a government of imbeciles. While Russia, in order to enslave Poland, compels her to speak Russian, while Germany prohibits French in the conquered provinces, your government endeavors to have you keep your own tongue, and you, in turn, an amazing people under an unbelievable government, you

---

[58] The comparison is not idle. On p. xxix of his introduction to *Noli Me Tangere*, Zea quotes from Unamuno's 'Elogio' the following: 'In the Philippines, as in my own Basque country, Spanish is a foreign language and of recent implantation . . . I learned to stammer in Spanish, and we spoke Spanish at home, but it was the Spanish of Bilbao, i.e. a poverty-stricken and timid Spanish. [Hence] we have been forced to remodel it, to forge by our efforts a language of our own. So it is that what in a certain respect is our weakness as writers is also our strength.'

insist on stripping yourselves of your own *nacionalidad*. One and all, you forget that so long as a people conserves its language, it also preserves the guarantee of its liberty, as a man his independence while he preserves his way of thinking. Language is the very thought [*pensamiento*] of a people.[59]

The tirade is powerful enough to let the reader forget that Ibarra-Simoun had an unscrupulous and cruel Basque grandfather, and that for purposes of his disguise affects a bad, heavily accented Tagalog; or that this denunciation of Hispanization is expressed in excellent Spanish. She might also overlook a contradictory argument of Simoun a few lines earlier: 'Do you want to add still one more language to the forty-odd already spoken in the islands so that you understand each other all the less?'[60] But the important thing is that Rizal never elsewhere wrote publicly in these vitriolic terms while in Europe—which would have appalled the comrades around *La Solidaridad*. In Spain he would have been speaking to the present, but transferred to Manila he is speaking to the future, with Poland and Alsace brought in as warnings.

Similar space-time shifts are visible as the novel moves towards its climax. After the campaign for a Spanish-language academy has failed, mysterious 'subversive' posters (*pasquinades*) appear all over the university one night, leading the regime to indiscriminate arrests—a clear replication of Cánovas's raids on the Central University of Madrid at the start of Rizal's senior year. The mysterious posters quickly cause a general panic, fed by wild rumours of insurrection and invasions of ferocious bandits, which recall the Mano Negra panic in Andalusia in 1883, and foreshadow the so-called 'revolutionary' peasant attack on Jerez early in 1892. It is interesting that Rizal anchors these plot developments in the Philippines by giving the relevant chapter the (untranslated) Tagalog title *Tatakut*, which means 'panic'.

Dansons la Ravachole

Finally, we come to Simoun's bomb-plot itself, which is to be accompanied by armed attacks by Tales' men and others outside the law, including

---

[59] *El Filibusterismo*, chapter VII ('Simoun'), p. 47. My rough translation; the original is not included here for reasons of space.

[60] '¿Queréis añadir un idioma más á los cuarenta y tantos que se hablan en las islas para entenderos cada vez menos?' *El Filibusterismo*, p. 47. There is as yet, evidently, no alternative national language. In Rizal's time Tagalog was understood only on the island of Luzon, and even there, only in the region around Manila.

a cruelly abused peninsular, who have agreed to coordinate with the mysterious jeweller. There are a number of curious features to this failed conspiracy. First, imagined in 1890–91, it precedes rather than follows the spectacular wave of bomb outrages that rocked Spain and France in 1892–94. From 1888 on, however, a growing number of explosions of bombs and petards had occurred, typically in industrial Barcelona, but also in Madrid, Valencia and Cádiz. Most were planted in factories, few caused loss of life or serious injuries, and almost none resulted in the unmasking of the perpetrators. There is every reason to suppose that they were arranged by angry workers under the influence of anarchist ideas, though perhaps some were organized by police agents-provocateurs. But the numbers of bombings and their gravity increased markedly after the 'Jerez Uprising' of January 8, 1892. That night, some 50–60 peasants entered the town to attack the prison where some of their comrades had earlier been incarcerated and tortured. It seems they expected, naïvely, that the local military garrison would support them. The police dispersed them, and it appeared that one peasant and two townspeople had been killed. Near the end of his third ministry, Cánovas launched an indiscriminate wave of repression against peasants and workers, and on February 10, four of the supposed leaders of the 'uprising' were publicly garrotted.[61]

A month later, a series of serious explosions started in Paris, the work of the half-Dutch, half-Alsatian François-Claude Koenigstein, better known as 'Ravachol', a criminal with a record of murder and robbery. He was quickly caught and put on trial. Claiming that he had acted in revenge for earlier violent police repression against a workers' demonstration in

---

[61] Nuñez Florencio, El Terrorismo, p. 49; Esenwein, Anarchist Ideology, pp. 175–80. Esenwein's excellent research has turned up some strange things. From one angle, the chain of events began with the Haymarket 'Riot' in Chicago at the beginning of May 1886. In an atmosphere of anti-'communist' and anti-immigrant hysteria, and after a travesty of a fair trial, four anarchists were hanged that November. The executions aroused indignation all over Europe (and of course also in the US), and on the initiative of French workers' organizations, May Day came to be celebrated annually (except in the US) in commemoration of the victims. The whole Spanish Left was a vigorous supporter of the new tradition, especially while Sagasta was still in power. Just after the May Day commemorations of 1891, two bombs exploded in Cádiz, killing one worker, and injuring several others. The local police arrested 157 people, but never found any provable perpetrator, so the possibility of agents-provocateurs cannot be ruled out. It was some of these prisoners whom the men of Jerez intended to liberate. The odd thing is that just at this juncture none other than Malatesta, accompanied by the rising anarchist intellectual star Tárrida del Mármol,

Clichy, followed by the trial of some workers at which the prosecutor demanded (but did not win) the death penalty, Ravachol told the court that he had acted on revolutionary anarchist principles. On July 11 he went to the guillotine shouting '*Vive l'Anarchie!*' and promising that his death would be avenged.[62] His was the first political execution in France since the massacres of the Communards.

In spite of his dubious past, Ravachol's death made him an instant hero of the *anarchisant* left on both sides of the Pyrenees. Núñez Florencio quotes a well-known popular song of the time, *La Ravachole*, as follows: *Dansons la Ravachole! / Vive le son, vive le son / Dansons la Ravachole / Vive le son / De l'explosion!* The famous theorist of anarchism, Elisée Reclus, was quoted in the Spanish anarchist press as saying that 'I am one of those who see in Ravachol a hero with a rare grandeur of spirit', while the writer Paul Adam, a member of Mallarmé's circle, wrote an *Éloge de Ravachol* in which he affirmed that 'Ravachol saw the suffering and misery of the people around him, and sacrificed his life in a holocaust. His charity, his disinterestedness, the vigour of his actions, his courage in the face of ineluctable death, raised him to the splendour of legend. In these times of cynicism and irony, a saint has been born to us.' The Spanish anarchist press described him as a 'violent Christ' and 'brave and dedicated revolutionary', and some anarchists put out two short-lived publications in his honour: *Ravachol* in late 1892 and *El Eco de Ravachol* early in 1893.[63]

---

was on a lecture and organizing tour of Spain, and was due to speak in Jerez. On hearing the news of the violent events, Malatesta rather courageously decided to keep going towards Cádiz, but disguised as a prosperous Italian businessman. He doesn't seem to have accomplished anything. Esenwein thinks it significant that neither at the time nor later did the anarchists proclaim January 8 as 'propaganda by the deed'. To the contrary, they always insisted that they had nothing to do with it.

[62] See Maitron, *Le Mouvement*, pp. 213–24. In his prison cell he told interviewers that he had lost his religious faith after reading Eugène Sue's *Le Juif errant!* Maitron points out that French anarchism in this period was largely a matter of tiny, clandestine or semi-clandestine units without real organizational ties between them. This characteristic made it hard for the police to monitor them effectively, and also made it relatively easy for criminal elements to penetrate them. French anarchism did not become a real political force till the end of the 1890s with the abandonment of propaganda by the deed, and the onset of syndicalism in working-class political life. Spanish anarchism had a much stronger and wider social foundation. That Ravachol was partly Alsatian is my deduction from the testimony of Ramón Sempau in his *Los Victimarios*, p. 15.

[63] Núñez Florencio, *El Terrorismo*, pp. 121–23.

The autumn of 1893 saw major repercussions of the Ravachol affair. On September 24, Paulino Pallás threw two bombs at the Captain-General of Catalonia, Gen. Arsenio Martínez Campos (signer of the Pact of Zanjón, which brought Céspedes's 10-year insurrection in Cuba to a peaceful end). This *attentat* resulted in one death, and several grave injuries (Campos was only scratched). Pallás made no attempt to hide or escape, but throwing his cap into the air, shouted '*Viva l'Anarquía!*' He was executed by firing squad a month later at the soon-to-be world-notorious fortress of Montjuich.[64] On November 7, the 32-year-old Salvador Santiago threw a huge bomb into the Barcelona Opera House during a performance of Rossini's *Guillermo Tel*, causing a large number of deaths and severe injuries among scores of the city's moneyed elite.[65] Many innocent suspects were arrested and tortured before Santiago was caught in hiding. After declaring he had acted to avenge Pallás, whom he knew and admired, he was garrotted at Montjuich on the 24th.[66] Martial

---

[64] For Spain, this was the first clear example of 'propaganda by the deed'. In October 1878 a young Catalan cooper called Juan Oliva had fired a gun at Alfonso XII but missed. A year later, the 19-year-old Francisco Otero tried to do the same, but proved an equally poor shot. Neither was connected to anarchist circles, and both were promptly executed. (Nuñez Florencio, *El Terrorismo*, p. 38.) Pallás was a poor young lithographer from Tarragon, who emigrated to Argentina; he married there, and then moved to Brazil in search of a better livelihood to support his family. He became a radical and anarchist while working as a typesetter in Santa Fé. On May Day 1892 he threw a petard into the Alcantara theatre in Rio shouting '*Viva l'Anarquía!*' No one was hurt, and the audience burst into cheers. When the Spanish police searched his house they found anarchist newspapers, a copy of Kropotkin's *The Conquest of Hunger*, and a lithograph of the Haymarket Martyrs. Most historians have argued that he acted partly out of indignation at the Jerez garrottings, but Nuñez Florencio says there is no document in Pallás's hand to support this claim. Compare Esenwein, *Anarchist Ideology*, pp. 184–5; Núñez Florencio, *El Terrorismo*, pp. 49, 53, and Maura, 'Terrorism', p. 130 (he says two were killed, and twelve wounded).

[65] The choice of this opera may not have been random. At its first 'convention' in 1879 Narodnaya Volya produced a programme that, *inter alia*, stated: 'We will fight with the means employed by Wilhelm Tell'. The legendary Swiss archer was widely regarded as an ancestral hero by late nineteenth-century radicals and nationalists. See Walter Laqueur, *A History of Terrorism*, rev. ed., New Brunswick, NJ 2002, p. 22.

[66] Santiago had started out as a Carlist and ardent Catholic, but poverty, petty crime (smuggling) and unpayable debts had aroused his interest in anarchism. Five other people were executed with him, though there is no convincing evidence that he did not, like Pallás, act on his own. See especially Esenwein, *Anarchist Ideology*, pp. 186–87 and Maura, 'Terrorism', p. 130. According to Bécarud and Lapouge, *Anarchistes*, p. 44, when he was asked what would happen to his daughters after his execution, Salvador Santiago said: 'If they are pretty, the bourgeois will take care of them.' Anarchist *boutade*? Or myth?

law was proclaimed in Barcelona by Sagasta (back in power since 1892), which lasted for a year. Its executor was none other than Weyler, just back from the Philippines. The anarchist press was forcibly shut down.

Then on December 9, Auguste Vaillant hurled a large bomb into the French Parliament, which fortunately killed no one, but wounded several of the deputies. On February 5 the next year, he was guillotined, the first instance in French memory of the death penalty in a case where no victim had been killed.[67] (President Sadi Carnot refused to commute the sentence, for which he was stabbed to death in Lyon, on June 24, 1894, by the young Italian anarchist Santo Jeronimo Cesario—who was guillotined two months later.) The culmination of this wave of anarchist bombs (though not its end by any means) came with a series of death-dealing explosions in Paris immediately following Vaillant's execution, and clearly in part to avenge him. The perpetrator was found to be Emile Henry, a young intellectual born in Spain to fleeing Communard exiles. He too was quickly caught, and guillotined on May 21.[68] For this study the single most important bombing did not come till the 'outrage' of Corpus Christi Day on June 7, 1896, in Barcelona—but this will be left for consideration in Part Three.

None of these five famous bombers of 1892–94 fit Simoun's personal profile. All of them were quite young, poor, half-educated (except for Henry), and self-proclaimed anarchists. None of their bombs had anything Huysmanesque about them, though Pallás is said to have used 'Fenian-type' bombs rather than the standard 'Orsini' model.[69] But consider some of the words that Emile Henry spoke at his trial, as reported by Joll. Asked why he had killed so many innocent people,

[67] Maitron says Vaillant came in handy for certain *dirigeants* of the Third Republic, who were reeling from public revelations about the Panama Canal Bubble scandal, and found him a wonderful way to shift public attention elsewhere—also to enact harsh laws against 'revolutionary propaganda' of any kind. *Le Mouvement*, p. 237.
[68] According to Joll, *The Anarchists*, p. 115, Henry was an outstanding student who got into the École Polytechnique, but then dropped out for the sake of anarchism. Clémenceau, deeply moved by Henry's execution, wrote: 'Henry's crime was that of a savage. But society's act seems to me a base revenge. Let the partisans of the death penalty go, if they have the courage, to sniff the blood at La Roquette [after 1851 the prison where all death sentences in Paris were carried out]. Then we shall talk . . .' Quoted in Maitron, *Le Mouvement*, p. 246.
[69] Núñez Florencio, *El Terrorismo*, p. 53, quoting a contemporary newspaper source. Felice Orsini (b. 1819) was a veteran of the 1848 revolutions, a deputy in the ephemeral Roman Republic, and a committed Italian nationalist. Imprisoned by the Austrian regime in the fortress of Mantua in 1855, he made a spectacular escape, and headed for Palmerston's England, where Mazzini was plotting insurrection

Henry replied sardonically that: '*il n'y a pas des innocents*' [There are no innocents]. Then:

> I was convinced that the existing organization [of society] was bad; I wanted to struggle against it so as to hasten its disappearance. I brought to the struggle a profound hatred, intensified every day by the revolting spectacle of a society where all is base, all is cowardly, where everything is a barrier to the development of human passions, to generous tendencies of the heart, to the free flight of thought . . . I wanted to show the bourgeoisie that their pleasures would be disturbed, that their golden calf would tremble violently on its pedestal, until the final shock would cast it down in mud and blood.

He went on to declare that anarchists

> do not spare bourgeois women and children, because the wives and children of those they love are not spared either. Are not those children innocent victims, who, in the slums, die slowly of anaemia because bread is scarce at home; or those women who grow pale in your workshops and wear themselves out to earn forty sous a day, and yet are lucky when poverty does not turn them into prostitutes; those old people whom you have turned into machines for production all their lives, and whom you cast on the garbage dump and the workhouse when their strength is exhausted. At least have the courage of your crimes, gentlemen of the bourgeoisie, and agree that our reprisals are fully legitimate . . .
>
> You have hanged men in Chicago, cut off their heads in Germany, strangled them in Jerez, shot them in Barcelona, guillotined them in Montbrisons and Paris, but what you will never destroy is anarchism. Its roots are too deep; it is born in the heart of a corrupt society which is falling to pieces; it is a violent reaction against the established order. It represents egalitarian and libertarian aspirations which are battering down existing authority; it is everywhere, which makes it impossible to capture. It will end by killing you.[70]

---

from seedy lodgings on the Fulham Road. His 1856 sensation, *The Austrian Dungeons in Italy*, quickly sold 35,000 copies, and his Byronic good looks and fervent rhetoric made him wildly popular on the lecture circuit. Meantime, he was inventing a new type of bomb, made mainly from fulminate of mercury, which did not need a fuse but exploded on impact. He tested it on a hut in Putney, and in disused quarries in Devonshire and Sheffield. Then, believing that the assassination of Louis Napoleon would spark a revolution in France, which would cause Italy to follow Paris's example, he crossed the Channel, and tried out his invention on January 14, 1858. His target was barely scratched but 156 people were injured, and eight eventually succumbed. Orsini was guillotined on March 13. Palmerston tried to pass a Conspiracy To Murder Bill, making plotting to murder foreign rulers a felony, but mishandled its passage, and was driven from office. See Jad Adams, 'Striking a Blow for Freedom', *History Today*, vol. 53, no. 9 (September 2003), pp. 18–19.

[70] Nuñez Florencio, *El Terrorismo*, p. 115–19. Note Henry's references to Jerez and Chicago, as well as Pallás and Vaillant.

Henry's rhetoric uncannily reproduces that of Simoun: hastening the rush of a corrupt system to the abyss, violent revenge against the ruling class, (including its 'innocents') for its crimes against the wretched and the poor, and the vision of an egalitarian and free society in the future.[71] Although Tagalog peasants had their own utopian and messianic traditions, embedded in folk-Catholicism,[72] Simoun's discourse does not reflect them but rather a language of European social fury that went back at least to the French Revolution, if not before, and was a special feature of anarchism in the era of 'propaganda by the deed'. But Simoun is imagined in a more complex, and also contradictory way. There is in him a negative photograph of Sue's aristocratic 'socialist' Rodolphe, who practices his own vigilante justice on evildoers and exploiters, of Huysmans's Des Esseintes adding one more enemy to a hideous society, and perhaps even Nechayev.[73] Much more important, however, is that Simoun is, in his own way, an anticolonial nationalist, who has national independence through 'revolution' on his mind; and his conspiracy is not just a symbolic moment of 'propaganda by the deed'.

---

[71] See 'Nitroglycerine in the Pomegranate', NLR 27, p. 109.

[72] The *locus classicus* is Reynaldo Clemeña Ileto, *Pasyón and Revolution: Popular Movements in The Philippines, 1840–1910*, Quezon City 1989.

[73] One should not rule Nechayev out. The pamphlet that he coauthored with Bakunin in 1869 was widely read all over Europe, and some of its themes seem echoed by Simoun in *El Filibusterismo*. In the issues of *La Solidaridad* of January 15 and 31, 1893, there is a curious two-part article, titled 'Una Visita', by Ferdinand Blumentritt, describing an unexpected visitor in the form of Simoun, who explains that Rizal had him appear to die in the novel to conceal from the colonial authorities his survival and his massive political multiplication among the Filipino population. A long and heated debate develops between them on the future of the Philippines, and on the methods to be pursued in the political struggle. At one point, the indignant ethnologist says: 'Mr Simoun, you are not merely a subversive, you are also a nihilist [Señor Simoun, usted es no solo filibustero sino también nihilista]'. To this, as he makes his mysterious departure, Simoun retorts sardonically: 'I am leaving for Russia, to enrol there in the school of the nihilists [Me marcho á Rusia para estudiar allí en la escuela de nihilistas]'! Nechayev had already died, aged only 35, in a tsarist prison the year before Rizal arrived in Europe. But Blumentritt was in some ways Rizal's closest friend, and I think it unlikely that he would have associated Simoun with Nihilism if the two had not discussed the latter seriously. Besides, Dostoevsky's *The Possessed* had come out in French translation in Paris in 1886, not long after Rizal had left the French capital for Germany and Blumentritt-in-Austria. We know also, thanks to De Ocampo that Rizal read (but when exactly?) Turgenev's *Fathers and Sons* in a German translation. (My thanks to Megan Thomas for bringing Blumentritt's odd articles to my attention.)

In the early 1890s, Filipinos and Cubans were especially well positioned to think along such lines, since they were subjected to the only European state which had by then lost 90 per cent of its imperium to independence movements. Simoun may speak scornfully of the Spanish Americas, but he understands a certain hope that their history opened up—which was not then available to the subjects of any other empire.

When Basilio—the young medical student recruited by Simoun after friars have killed his little brother and driven his mother insane—learns of the 'infernal machine' inside the pomegranate lamp with which Simoun intends to blow up the colonial elite, Captain-General included, at the wedding party, he exclaims: 'But what will the world say at the sight of such carnage?' Simoun replies:

> The world will applaud as always, legitimizing the more powerful and the more violent. Europe applauded when the nations of the West sacrificed the lives of millions of *indios* in America, and definitely not in order to found other nations far more moral or peace-loving. Yonder stands the North, with its egoistic liberty, its Lynch law, its political manipulations; yonder stands the South with its turbulent republics, its barbarous revolutions, its civil wars, and its pronunciamentos, like its mother Spain! Europe applauded when a powerful Portugal plundered the Moluccas, and [now] applauds as England destroys in the Pacific region the local primitive races in order to implant that of its own emigrants. Europe will applaud [us], as it applauds the end of a drama, the denouement of a tragedy. The common people barely notice the bases of what is happening, they simply observe its effects![74]

After the us, Colombia, Argentina, and Paraguay have had their independence applauded (accepted) by Europe, so to speak, why not the Philippines and Cuba? In these sentences, one feels how much closer to the Philippines of the 1890s were Mexico and Peru than were Tonkin

---

[74] Basilio: '¿Qué dira el mundo, á la vista de tanta carnicería?' Simoun: 'El mundo aplaudirá como siempre, dando la razón al más fuerte, al más violente! . . . Europa ha aplaudido cuando las naciones del occidente sacrificaron en América millones de indios y no por cierto para fundar naciones mucho más morales ni más pacíficas; allí está el Norte con su libertad egoista, su ley de Lynch, sus engaños políticos; allí está el Sur con sus repúblicas intranquilas, sus revoluciones bárbaras, guerras civiles, pronunciamentos, como en su madre España! Europa ha aplaudido cuando la poderosa Portugal despojó á las islas Molucas, aplaude cuando Inglaterra destruye en el Pacífico las razas primitivas para implantar la de sus emigrados. Europa aplaudirá como se aplaude al fin de un drama, al fin du una tragedia; el vulgo se fija poco en el fondo, sola mira el efecto!' *El Filibusterismo*, chapter XXIII ('La Ultima Razón [The Final Argument]'), p. 250.

and Java. In effect, a successful insurrection was quite possible in the Philippines. And indeed, four months before Rizal's death, Andrés Bonifacio began one on the outskirts of Manila—a bare eighteen months after Martí led the way in Cuba.

An enigmatic smile

This brings us to one last curious aspect of *El Filibusterismo*. The novel's final pages are filled with a lengthy dialogue between the dying Simoun and the gentle native priest, Father Florentino, with whom he has found temporary refuge. Simoun poses the question of Ivan Karamazov. He says that if *vuestro Dios* demands such inhuman sacrifices, such humiliations, tortures, expropriations, misery and exploitation of the good and innocent, telling them simply to suffer and to work, 'What kind of God is this?'—'¿*Qué Dios es ése?*'[75] He says no more, while the old priest tells him that God understands all Simoun's sufferings and will forgive him, but that he has chosen evil methods to achieve worthy ends, and this is inadmissible. Most commentators have assumed that the old priest represents Rizal's last word on the politico-moral drama of the novel, and find their views reinforced by the fact that (as we shall see in Part Three) Rizal refused to have anything to do with Bonifacio's conspiracy—even though it was made in his name—and indeed denounced it. But to make this judgement so easily requires overlooking a strange brief chapter near the end, called 'El Misterio', of whose seven pages in the original manuscript three were blacked out by the author.

We are in the house of the rich Orenda family, at which three callers have arrived, in the chaotic aftermath of the failed explosion and armed incursions. One of the visitors is the young blade Momoy (suitor of the eldest Orenda daughter Sensia), who attended the fateful wedding party of Paulita Gomez and was a befuddled witness to what happened. Another is the student Isagani who, to save Paulita's life, had seized the lethal lamp and plunged into the Pasig river with it. Momoy tells the family that an unknown robber ran off with the lamp, before diving into the water. Sensia breaks in to say, quite remarkably: 'A robber? A member of the Black Hand? [*Un ladrón? Uno de la Mano Negra?*]' No one knows, Momoy continues, whether he was a Spaniard, a Chinese, or an *indio*. The third visitor, a silversmith who helped do the wedding decorations, adds that

---

[75] *El Filibusterismo*, chapter xxxix (untitled), p. 283.

the rumour is that the lamp was on the verge of exploding and the house of the bride was also mined with gunpowder. Momoy is stunned and panic-stricken at this, and by his expression shows his fear. Then, seeing that Sensia has noticed, and mortified in his masculinity: '"What a shame!" he exclaimed with an effort, "How the robber bungled it! All would have been killed . . ."'. The women are completely petrified. Then:

> "It is always wrong to seize something which does not belong to one", said Isagani with an enigmatic smile. "If the robber had known what it was all about, and if he had been able to reflect upon it, he certainly would not have done what he did." And, after a pause, he added: "I would not be in his place for anything in the world."

An hour later, he takes his leave to 'retire permanently' in the household of his uncle (Father Florentino, the native priest at the dying Simoun's side), and disappears from the novel.[76] The goodhearted, patriotic student, who has never smiled enigmatically before, regrets that he wrecked Simoun's scheme. The Spanish makes it clear that 'permanently (por siempre)' is merely his intention at the moment of departure. It is as if the reader is invited to await a sequel to El Filibusterismo.

We are now perhaps in a better to position to understand both the proleptic character of the novel, and the significance of Rizal's terming it a Filipino novel. Technically the prolepsis is engineered by a massive transfer of events, experiences and sentiments from Spain to the Philippines, which then appear as shadows of an imminent future; their imminence is in turn guaranteed by a firm location in the time of Captain-General Weyler, who was still in power when the book came out. Contextually, the future emerges both from the past and the present in a different sense. The Spanish Empire had always been primarily American, and its virtual evaporation between 1810 and 1830 promised a final liquidation to the residues, while also proffering warnings of the consequences of prematurity. Europe itself, Rizal thought, was menaced by a vast conflagration, conflicts among its warring powers, but also by violent movement from below. El Filibusterismo was written

---

[76] '¡Qué lastima! exclamó haciendo un esfuerzo; qué mal ha hecho el ladrón! Hubieran muerto todos . . .' 'Siempre es malo apoderarse de lo que no es suyo, contestó Isagani con enigmática sonrisa; si ese ladrón hubiese sabido de qué se trataba y hubiese podido reflexionar, de seguro que no lo habría hecho. Y añadió despues de una pausa: Por nada del mundo quisiera estar en su lugar'. El Filibusterismo, pp. 271–72.

from the wings of a global proscenium on which Bismarck and Vera Zasulich, Yankee manipulations and Cuban insurrections, Meiji Japan and the British Museum, Huysmans and Mallarmé, Catalonia and the Carolines, Kropotkin and Salvador Santiago, all had their places. *Cochers* and 'homeopathists' too.

In late 1945, a bare two months after the Japanese Occupation of his country had collapsed, but Dutch colonialism had yet to return in force, Indonesia's young, first Prime Minister, Sutan Sjahrir, described the condition of his revolution-starting countrymen as *gelisah*. This is not a word that is easily translated into English: one has to imagine a semantic range covering 'feverish', 'anxious', 'restless', 'unmoored', and 'expectant'. This is the feel of *El Filibusterismo*. Something is coming.

REVIEWS

One China, Many Paths, edited by Chaohua Wang
Verso: London 2003, £20, hardback
368 pp, 1 85984 537 1

ARIF DIRLIK

CHINA'S CRITICAL INTELLIGENTSIA

While contemporary Chinese readers, Wang Chaohua observes in her introduction to this selection of essays,

> have access in their native language to large areas of Western literature and
> philosophy, political and economic thought, to classical texts and contem-
> porary ideas of the world . . . this process of cultural familiarization has
> been one-sided. Neither the length and depth of traditional Chinese civiliza-
> tion, nor the importance of China in the modern history of the world, are
> reflected in a comparable range of Western translations of Chinese thought
> and culture.

Her aim in this volume 'is to help in a modest way to correct this imbalance, by presenting the diversity of outlook among contemporary Chinese
thinkers directly'.

Few would dispute Wang's observation, although what she has to say,
and the manner in which it is said, bears further reflection; I will return to it
below. The undertaking itself is to be commended without reservation. One
China, Many Paths joins a growing list of publications seeking to acquaint
English-speaking readers with developments in the PRC through the works
of Chinese intellectuals themselves. Whereas most previous volumes have
concentrated on culture and cultural analysis, however, Wang's collection
stands out for its focus on issues of democracy and social justice, as seen
by a varied and distinguished group of Chinese thinkers. It is an important

contribution, both in introducing public intellectuals quite well-known in Chinese circles to the Anglophone world and in making available a body of writings on issues of utmost concern to critics of the developmentalist path on which the Chinese Communist Party has launched the country.

These concerns no doubt relate to Wang's own experience. Born in Beijing she is, like many of the writers in this volume, a graduate of 1989, but one who had been formed politically and intellectually during the more radical days of the Cultural Revolution. She became a leader of the student movement in Tiananmen Square, confronting Premier Li Peng on national television. After the military crackdown of June 4th she was one of the two women on the most-wanted list broadcast by the government in the drag-net that followed. After eight months in hiding she reached America, where she is now an essayist and student of Chinese literature at UCLA. Most of her contributors are also among the older *alumnae* of 1989, born in the 1950s; their differences have been magnified significantly since then with the rapid changes in Chinese society—most importantly, the dizzying incorporation into global capitalism following Deng Xiaoping's famous imperial tour of the South in 1992, and the structural transformations it has wrought both at home and in the PRC's relationship to the world at large.

Following a suggestion by Wang Hui—the best known of these intellectuals in North America and Europe, whose interview leads the volume—Wang establishes a loose parallel between the 1980s and 1990s, and the two decades that followed the May Fourth Movement of 1919: in each case, a decade of euphoria and intellectual excitement is succeeded by one of intellectual sobriety, introspection and complexity, with the passage between them marked by a traumatic event—the Guomindang suppression of the revolutionary movement in 1927, and the Tiananmen Massacre of 1989. She is aware nevertheless of the limits of such analogies—which, as so often, may say more about the self-image of those making them than about the historical realities of changing intellectual moods, or the relationship of one period to the other. For all the euphoric embrace of new cultural currents from abroad (the so-called 'culture fever'), the 1980s were infused by the deep anxieties created by post-revolutionary uncertainties that were sustained—as they still are, if to a lesser extent—by bouts of repression or relaxation from above. June 1989 was a surprise only to those who had come to believe in their own illusions about Deng's reforms. In fact, the issues of culture and society that exercised intellectuals in the 1980s had more in common with the debates on modernity in the 1930s.

On the other hand, the greater complexity of intellectual and cultural exploration in the 1990s has been accompanied by serious doubts about the value of such activity, in a society which—at least in major centres like Shanghai, Beijing and Guangzhou—has come to assume all the trappings

REVIEW

of advanced consumerism, albeit surrounded by intensifying poverty and inequality. Intellectuals have recovered from the severe marginalization and impoverishment they experienced in the first half of the 1990s. But like their peers elsewhere, they now face the twin challenges of their own class devaluation and the commodification of intellectual life. Wang is correct to point to the two trends that have set the context for these exchanges since the turn of the century: the emergence of a transborder 'Chinese space of discussion', which calls into question the actual relationship of intellectuals to the society they write about; and the growing professionalization of university life which, within the context of cultural commodification, raises serious questions about the possibility of critical work. What makes these issues more urgent is that the same trends have also opened discussions in the PRC to fleeting fashions from abroad.

In the 1980s, intellectual and cultural work in the PRC was largely shaped by an urge to escape an oppressive socialist legacy. With integration into the global economy, rapid development and the increasingly open identification of the Communist Party with capitalism, the legacies left behind by the socialist revolutionary past have begun to appear in a more positive light, dividing intellectuals in new ways. A basic goal of *One China, Many Paths* is to convey a sense of these differences, and of the broad political spectrum into which critical intellectual life has been diffracted by traumatic events and social change. The collection reveals eloquently the common concerns that drive politically-engaged intellectual work in the PRC, as well as the disagreements over solutions that divide the thinkers themselves.

Wang's introduction gives a summary but useful history of developments on the Chinese intellectual scene over the decade and a half since 1989. The 'new left' versus 'liberal' division that had emerged by the late 1990s also, to a certain extent, characterizes the selections in this volume. Five of the contributors—Wang Hui, Gan Yang, Wang Xiaoming, Qian Liqun and Li Changping—can be situated on the 'left' side of the political spectrum, Wang suggests; and six—Zhu Xueqin, Qin Hui, He Qinglian, Xiao Xuehui and Wang Yi—on the 'liberal' side; while Chen Pingyuan, Wang Anyi and Hu Angang 'would probably disavow any leaning to one or the other'. The labels are very tentative: there is much overlap between the positions, which share a critical attitude toward recent developments in Chinese society but otherwise range over a broad political spectrum. In Part One, which consists of four long interviews, the new left and liberal perspectives are strongly articulated by Wang Hui and Zhu Xueqin, respectively—two prominent representatives of these positions. Chen Pingyuan voices the concerns of a writer bent on reaffirming the importance of scholarship, as against general intellectual work. This was also a point of departure for Wang Hui and others in the journal *Xueren* ('scholar') in the early 1990s, and has been one moment in the revival of interest in the nationalistically oriented *Guoxue* ('national studies') since 1993. The interview with Qin Hui, who teaches history at Tsinghua, offers an impressive analysis of social and political inequality in the PRC, theoretically incisive and with a broad range of historical comparison—Ancient Greece and Rome, Russia, China, Europe; he is perhaps better described as an independent socialist/populist than as liberal in political orientation.

Part Two deals with social issues. It is interesting, and revealing, that three of the four contributions here are by writers that Wang would classify as 'liberal'. He Qinglian, whose seminal and initially proscribed book, *Modernization's Pitfalls*, launched a wave of social criticism, provides a concise analysis of an emergent class structure in the PRC—as with several of the texts, this was first presented in English in NLR. The essays by Wang Yi, Hu Angang and Li Changping offer sharp critiques of corruption and the plunder of resources by a political elite that has benefited enormously from the privatization of public property which it engineered—as well as from the intensifying exploitation of workers and peasants in the name of the superiority of socialist developmental efficiency.

Cultural questions are addressed in Part Three, with Xiao Xuehui offering a spirited polemic on the 'industrialization' of education with, once again, efficiency as the fetishized goal. Wang Xiaoming's 'Manifesto of Cultural Studies' engages in a sustained critique of the 'new ideology' as camouflage for social ills, and on the commodification of culture. The well-known novelist Wang Anyi is the only one to address issues of gender, although her criticisms of modernity and globalization are unfortunately too cursory to add much to the substance gathered here. Gan Yang, whose writings in the 1980s gained him considerable popularity, considers in a somewhat uninspired essay the prospects for party politics and constitutional government in China, in the light of US experience—federalism, or a unified state? A remarkable piece by Qian Liqun takes up the revolutionary legacy in Chinese thought, including that of Mao Zedong, which he colourfully describes as 'a fruit hard to consume, but impossible to discard'. Finally, Part Four consists of a three-way discussion on desirable futures for the PRC between Wang Chaohua and two other prominent graduates of Tiananmen, Wang Dan and Li Minqi. Li Minqi's explicitly Marxist analysis finds a counterpart in Wang Dan's liberalism, while Wang Chaohua's own position, somewhere between the two, reveals the limitations of the terms, left and liberal, within this context.

In Wang Hui's distinction, 'liberals want to separate the political and economic realms, whereas we argue that the problems of each are intertwined—you cannot always distinguish between them, or say which is more decisive'. The intellectuals associated with the 'new left' in this volume are critical of the developmentalist fetishism that infuses the thinking of the current CCP leadership, and of incorporation into global capitalism motivated by neoliberal teleologies; of the ideological cover-up of new social problems, especially in the countryside, and of the commodification of everyday life. At the same time, they are unwilling to abandon the legacies of the Revolution, including those of Mao Zedong, or to give up on a search for 'alternative' modernities. 'Liberals', on the other hand, stress the distorting effects of Communist Party dictatorship on economic and social change, and seek solutions to the problems produced by development in its elimination. Zhu Xueqin sums up: 'The principal reason for the divergence between liberals and the new left is clear: while the latter focus on criticizing the market system, the former call for reform of the political system. This is the root of the difference between the two.'

Whether or not this adds up to a refusal to recognize a relationship between politics and the economy, as Wang Hui suggests, is another matter. The selections identified with the liberal camp are most impressive for their condemnation not only of the absence of democracy but also for the deepening social injustices in their country. Xu Ming, general editor of the 'China's Problems' series which published the mainland edition of He Qinglian's *Modernization's Pitfalls* (and a liberal by the logic of either Wang Hui or Zhu Xueqin) once told me that he and his group were the 'true Marxists' in the PRC—from a perspective that sees in Marxism a theoretical justification for the determination of the social and the political by the economic. On this view, it follows that the full realization of the free-market system is the precondition for political transformation and the alleviation of social inequality. The free-market system is what a radical Marxism challenges, of course, and this is the point of departure for China's new left. They also pay closer attention to issues of power and the multinationals' domination within a globalizing capitalism. Liberals invested much hope in strategies of privatization and in China's structural incorporation into the global economy. With the admission of the PRC into the WTO and the recent sell-offs, both these demands are being realized—neutralizing important liberal criticisms of the CCP. These developments will test liberal solutions to problems of democracy and social injustice. For the time being, of course, democracy in the PRC is still far distant; and if the consequences of neoliberalism elsewhere provide any evidence, the achievement of social justice through incorporation into the global market is likely to remain the most utopian of goals.

What is interesting is that economic development over the last decade has brought forth its own problems. Chinese intellectuals can once again speak to issues of political democracy and social justice, appealing in the process to positions that were suspect only a few years ago because of their association with 'conservatism' in the CCP. Nor should the labels that these thinkers may attach to one another be allowed to obscure the complexities of the intellectual scene, or the radical transfigurations of left, liberal or even conservative politics in a post-socialist intellectual environment, still dominated by a Communist Party bent on carrying the country into capitalism in the name of an ever-more distant Communism. It is the left here that is most critical of the CCP in the name of democracy and social justice, as in the questions it raises about the preoccupation with globalization from the mid-1990s. Liberals—critical of the neoliberals who are influential in economic policy-making but otherwise quite happy to accommodate political despotism—focus rather on the reform of the political system which they hope will not only bring democracy but also alleviate social injustice. Conservatives (not represented in this volume) are bent on reviving national traditions, but are anxious to articulate these within the parameters of 'socialism with Chinese characteristics'.

Further complications emerge in the preoccupation with 'globalization' from the late 1990s, simultaneous with the increased visibility of the liberal–new left split—which may itself perhaps be viewed as a manifestation of the effects of globalization within Chinese thought. Beginning with the Jiang–Zhu leadership, and continuing under Hu Jintao and Wen Jiabao, the Party-State in the PRC has been committed not just to opening the country to global capitalism—as with incorporation in the WTO—but also to projecting national power on the world scene, exemplified by the 2008 Beijing Olympics, among other things. Liberal cosmopolitanism and new left 'nationalism' are entangled in broader issues of national development, power and identity that endow their politics with considerable instability. This context, too, is important in grasping the meanings the various political labels carry in Chinese intellectual life.

Any selection of this kind is easily faulted for favouring certain trends over others. Given the complexities of the rapidly changing intellectual landscape in the PRC, it would be difficult to put together a collection truly representative of the scene as a whole. Still, the editor could have been more explicit in spelling out the orientation of the volume and its goals. On a technical note, given the rapidity of changes in the PRC over the last decade and a half, when and where an essay was first published has some importance. This information is missing from a number of the essays, especially unpublished articles or those first circulated on the internet. 'Intellectual distinction and political representation', which the editor took as the primary criteria of selection for the volume, are not guarantees in conveying a comprehensive or unbiased sense of the intellectual scene in the PRC. The first is a matter of judgement, and is not in itself an indicator of public influence. Neither does the political range represented here by any means exhaust that of Chinese intellectual life. Wang Chaohua herself notes several absences, from technocratic intellectuals to representatives of nationalities. We could add: neoliberals, cultural conservatives, cultural and economic globalizers, ecologists and Party intellectuals (not just intellectuals in the Party, as many are, but those involved in bringing new ideas and orientations into the ccp). Fortuitously, the writers here are well distributed in terms of their geographical origins, but there is little virtue attached to this since most now operate out of the major centres, Beijing or Shanghai. There is no explicit effort at regional representation *per se*, which should be crucial since inequalities among intellectuals are very much a function of current location, much more important than original birthplace in terms of the hearing they are given on the national (and international) scene. Finally, as noted, the editor points out that intellectual space no longer corresponds to national boundaries, especially with the increasing importance of the internet. Overseas intellectuals are participants in these discussions and, though there may be practical reasons for excluding them—their writings are already available in English, for example—the overall consequence is to distort the context of the debate.

Despite the importance of the questions of democracy and social justice that are the focus here, it should also be noted that this selection ignores, in its preoccupation with things Chinese, the silence of Chinese intellectuals on global issues of the utmost significance—which may go a long way toward explaining why they have not acquired much visibility or significance on the international intellectual scene. One point here is that intellectuals of whatever stripe are not immune to the pressures of their social environment. It is remarkable how easily many in China, especially in the major urban centres and institutions, have slipped back into elite roles, following the economic deprivation in the early 1990s. In some cases, this has been facilitated by grants from overseas, including European, us and Japanese sources. A sociology of intellectuals may be crucial to understanding their cultural production and *One China, Many Paths* could have devoted closer attention to this problem, if only to bring out the increasing resemblances between the intellectual scene in China and elsewhere.

The other issue is the asymmetry in native-language access to Chinese or Euro-American thought, one to which I referred at the beginning of this essay. Wang's criticism is a common one, echoing for example Theodore Huters,'who writes in his introduction to Wang Hui's *China's New Order* that 'it has long been a matter of concern among Chinese of even modest educational attainment that there is a far greater attention to and knowledge about the West among ordinary Chinese than there is awareness of China among Westerners'. The point has often been made with respect to inequalities between the us and Europe and the Third World. It is not that the First World does not know about the Third; arguably, in certain respects the First World knows more about the Third than the latter knows about itself. The question is rather: who knows, what kind of knowledge and to what end? What is missing in most instances is interest in other ways of knowing. What Chinese thinkers have to say may matter to China specialists, but it would be hard to argue that it is of general intellectual interest—and the specialists themselves may have something to gain from exaggerating the contributions of Chinese intellectuals to contemporary thought, which may in fact add up to little more than the transfer of the Gao Xingjian syndrome in literature to the realms of social criticism and philosophy.

Colonial legacies of power are important to this asymmetrical relationship, as is the ideological hegemony that continues to underwrite them. It is also necessary to note what I would describe as the 'Middle Kingdom' mentality that continues to prevail among Chinese intellectuals—not in the ordinary misleading usage of a haughty disregard for the world, but rather in the sense of an obsessive and narrowly conceived preoccupation with China and its relationship to the 'West'. The reluctance of Chinese intellectuals to speak on general world issues, even as the PRC is headed for world-power status, is a striking characteristic of most of their writing. So is the exclusive China–West focus, commonplace in these discussions, which suggests obliviousness to the world that exists outside of a China–West space—one that reifies both China and the West, even among confirmed deconstructionists and postmodernists. Ironically, conferences on globalization (which have become a minor industry in the PRC) also remain trapped within this particular matrix and are generally restricted to participants from China, North America and Europe, not even extending to neighbouring societies, let alone more remote Third World nations. Many Chinese intellectuals, in other words, are complicit in the fetishization of Euro-America and the legitimization of the power relationships they would criticize. They contribute, in their own way, to the perpetuation of inequalities in world knowledge, not just between Euro-America and China, but also between China and the rest of the world. This is quite a difference from the radical past when, whatever the realities, Chinese intellectuals at least aspired to challenge intellectual and cultural disparities, within a revolutionary society that sought to transform global class-power relations. It *is* important for the world to have access to the thinking of Chinese intellectuals; in overcoming Euro-American hegemony, it is equally important for PRC intellectuals to engage a world of culture and ideas that is not bound by inherited geographies of power.

It is not only intellectuals in the PRC who are oblivious to this problem, but also PRC promoters in the US and Europe, who seem to be constitutionally incapable of accepting that China is just like any other society which, in the particular mode of its escape from domination, visits devastation on others. It is important, not just for the PRC but for the world at large, that the country be 'worlded'. *One China, Many Paths* offers examples of the kind of thinking associated with the most progressive sectors in the PRC. It also provides eloquent testimonial to the limitations set by past and present hegemonies on Chinese thinkers' abilities to provide intellectual leadership on a host of contemporary problems that are not just Chinese but global in both their sources and their consequences. There are writers who are willing to challenge US depredations on the global scene and oppose the legacies of colonialism. Their voices are heard in this volume only marginally, as most of the contributors are preoccupied with questions of left or centrist liberalism, in which the radical inheritance of the past appears merely as a spectral presence, desubstantiated in its translation into the language of academic politics.

Contemporary Chinese intellectuals face problems produced by a specific social and political environment, but they also confront many of the same questions as the rest of us, even if they encounter them under different circumstances. We need to recognize the ways in which they have been repeatedly abused for daring to be social critics, or just for being different. It is equally important not to let memories of political repression stand in the way of efforts to expand the realm of freedom in the future, when past experiences may in fact catapult Chinese intellectuals to the forefront of struggles for greater liberties. They, in turn, have to learn to speak in another language, not just the language of nations and states, but the language of democracy and justice that has a relevance beyond Chinese political and cultural boundaries. The thinkers in this volume speak in such a language. But to achieve the well-deserved recognition of their activities as critical intellectuals, they need to make a greater effort at overcoming their self-imposed limitations in participating in the global (not just 'Western') dialogue.

Alex Woloch, *The One vs the Many: Minor Characters and the Space of the Protagonist in the Novel*
Princeton University Press 2003, $21.95, paperback
391 pp, 0 69111 314 9

RACHEL MALIK

'WE ARE TOO MENNY'

Character is an unfashionable subject within the current *doxa* of literary studies, and one of the many strengths of Alex Woloch's study is his una-bashed facing of the problem head-on. Naïve responses that treat characters as people and pay no attention to the processes of representation are easy targets; but the seemingly non-gullible alternatives are, for Woloch, equally evasive. Character cannot be reduced to theme, or rhetorical figure, or an action-potential within the plot, any more than it can be simply read off (and perhaps seen off) as an ideological position. Such strategies should always be part of how we read character, but they do not, on their own, grapple with the anthropomorphism of characters, who so often seem to exist beyond the repertoire of gestures, actions, thoughts and words in which they are inscribed. Character is a myth in Barthes's sense (though Woloch himself treats Barthes rather peremptorily), and must be read as at once true and unreal. We need to accept the true force of character: why readers can treat characters as people (or even intimates), speculating about their pre-and-post narrative 'lives'. But we must also explain it, as a constituent and effect of the textual process.

The place of minor characters, from Dickens's memorable 'gargoyles' (as Orwell termed them) to the blank servants behind 'dinner was served', lay bare the problem of character most acutely, and Woloch rejects a wide variety of critical responses in forging his own argument about them. Minor characters cannot be conceived as a failure of representation—the static, even stuffed, quality of 'Austen's men' would be one example. Nor can they be written off as not meriting the attention that the protagonist deserves. Minor characters cannot be viewed exclusively as foils for major characters, as figures for the protagonist's dilemmas or unconscious desires (though they often also function in this way). Nor are minor characters 'really' major characters: Bertha Mason is not the 'real' heroine of *Jane Eyre*. This is not a book about unsung heroes but rather about the processes of 'unsinging'. Woloch insists on minor characters as just that. His concern is with the literary processes—distortion, compression, dispatch—that constitute them as minor, or 'flat' (a term he develops from Forster). In one of many brilliantly defamiliarizing moments, Woloch defines the undeveloped minor character as one whose subjectivity has not been fully 'effaced'. The protagonist's interest, the way that narrative attention is distributed and redistributed, is as much a *formal* as an ethical question. And whilst minor characters may function as (developmental) foils to the protagonist, such formulas resist the fundamental interdependency of the two.

For Woloch, the emergence of a central protagonist as a self-reflective consciousness in the realist novel is structured by the 'minoring' or *subordination* of other characters within the narrative structure. The many varieties of minor character who jostle for attention, from the rigorously constrained parodies of Austen to Dickens's compressed grotesques, are the necessary textual effects of the protagonist's rich and complex interiority, so strongly marked in the classic fiction of this period. *The One vs the Many* explores an epoch—between about 1810 and 1865—of general novelistic innovation, centring on three writers—Austen, Dickens and Balzac—who, for Woloch, are explicitly interested in the narrative questions posed by character. His thesis calls for a very detailed mapping of character relations, and three of his four main chapters are devoted to close studies of single novels: *Pride and Prejudice*, *Great Expectations* and *Le Père Goriot*. These are complemented by a number of fascinating excursuses, on Henry James, George Eliot, Shakespeare, Sophocles and the *Iliad*; a roll-call which summons up Auerbach's *Mimesis*, an important intertext for Woloch's book.

The structural dialectic between major and minor is clearly demonstrated in Woloch's probing and original account of Austen's *Pride and Prejudice*. Elizabeth's emergence as the protagonist, which is not a given at the outset, is only possible through the 'minoring' of those around her, and in particular her four sisters. Her coming-to-be as a reflective and critical agent, as a *rounded* character, has as its necessary counterpart, the flattening and subordination of others. Elizabeth's judgements of her family and, crucially a less stable and circumscribed acquaintance, enable her to extract and abstract social characteristics. This process of exacting evaluation simultaneously constructs her fullness, as a thinking, conscious being and delimits and distorts the social world around her, creating an asymmetry or imbalance between characters which becomes a typical structure for the nineteenth-century novel.

REVIEW

It is in this context that we can start to make sense of Woloch's argument that 'minor characters are the proletariat of the novel' and his concepts of character-space and character-system. The rounded character is not a naïvely imputed individual but the liberal subject inscribed in the Rights of Man. The asymmetry produced by the dialectic of round and flat is the registration of both the possible completeness of all, and the knowledge that individual development is achievable only at the necessary cost of the subordination of the many. Character-space is the intersection between this inherent individual potential and the determined space of the narrative as a whole; the character-system is the arrangement of these 'multiple and differentiated character-spaces'. Elizabeth's emergence as the protagonist, distinguishable from her sisters and from the blur of other young women, is predicated on the marriage market, where the general instability of social relations in the late eighteenth and early nineteenth century is especially acute. For Woloch, this context is played out in the conflict between an individual marriage plot of which Elizabeth is the chief beneficiary, and the insecurities and dangers governing the marriage market as a whole. One woman's security is gained at the cost of potentially uncountable others—the many. The two most important minor characters, Elizabeth's youngest and most irresponsible sister, Lydia, and the seducer-adventurer Wickham, embrace the dangers of this larger social world and, for Woloch, represent the forces of social multiplicity that threaten the protagonist but are convincingly constrained by the end of the novel.

Competition is also a central feature in Woloch's analyses of Dickens and Balzac's *Père Goriot*, where he binds the various modes of being major and minor more explicitly to the relations between capital and labour. In *Pride and Prejudice*, Elizabeth's interiority emerges in the narrative process of the novel, which itself dramatizes the coming-to-be of the protagonist. For Dickens, in contrast, the novelistic protagonist is always already a given. Dickens is interesting to Woloch because the often weak protagonist's interiority is threatened by social exteriority and, above all, multiplicity. In *Great Expectations*, Pip is frequently silenced, confused, and even overwhelmed by his encounters with others. In becoming a gentleman, Pip is bound inextricably to a seemingly endless chain of subordinated others: from lawyers and clerks to tailors and servers. Distorted, compressed, and frequently only ever half-visible, these minor characters are the necessary condition of Pip's development, his *Bildung*, and in turn gesture to the greater multitude of the modern industrial city that can never be fully grasped. Distortion and flatness become so extreme that they become foregrounded: 'the minor character's significance rests in—not against—his insignificance; his strange prominence is inseparable from his obscurity'.

Through his analysis of Dickens, Woloch identifies the two types of minor character who 'people' the novels of the period: the worker and the eccentric. Both are read as embedded in a variety of discourses about the urban industrial working class (Engels, Marx, Mayhew). The minor character as a narrative worker is distorted, just as labour is reduced to its minimum functionality for maximum efficiency. The gallery of Dickensian characters, compressed to a series of repetitious phrases, gestures, actions, is a particularly clear instance. The eccentric minor character is the other side of the coin: the working-class dissipation and criminality suppressed and constituted by functionality that always threaten to overturn a precarious social and narrative order. In narrative terms, eccentrics explode into the text, disordering it: Bertha Mason in *Jane Eyre* is a defining case. In *Great Expectations*, Pip is bound to both types; most specifically, his wealth is predicated on the criminality that banished his benefactor Magwitch to Australia to make his millions. Within this socio-narrative context, Woloch argues that Magwitch's homecoming represents the worker returning to claim the wealth he has produced. There is something to be said for this thesis, for Magwitch has certainly made Pip. But this argument can only be pressed so far, for Magwitch has done what labour cannot—accumulate capital. And in winning his passport out of the doomed repetitive time of the Dickensian worker-character, he changes.

Woloch's limited reading of Magwitch is in part an effect of his limited engagement with the *temporal* dimensions that shape character. This is predominantly a book about space: character-space, the processes of compression and expansion, and the dangers of overcrowding (though it is surprising that Woloch only considers the crowd as it is figured in particular characters, and not representations of *collective* agency as such). Woloch seems to equate Dickens's distinctive, partly obscured vision of the many exclusively with their overwhelming quantity. But the constitutive distortion of minor characters is also shaped by an attempt to record the *accelerated* quality of modern life: a few words scrawled in a notebook before the subject vanishes. Poe dramatizes this acceleration in *The Man of the Crowd*, where the narrator's pursuit of an unclassifiable figure generates a feverish energy and exhaustion as he rushes after him through the night. Think also of the technological apparatus brought to bear by the forces of good to capture that quintessentially modern monster, Dracula: shorthand and stenograph. Dracula not only wants to 'pass' in the metropolitan crowd, he is energized by it and, perversely of course, rejuvenated by the sheer pace of modernity.

In Balzac's *Père Goriot* likewise, the unique, developmental time of Rastignac, the ambitious young man from the rural South (and one of the possible protagonists), is constantly undermined by the Parisian *everyday*, where everyone's life proceeds according to type as a repetition of someone else's story. Balzac completes the elegant scheme of Woloch's argument. In Austen the idea of the protagonist is in the making, and its achievement is the constraining of the many; in Dickens the novelistic protagonist is an established category but vulnerable to social multiplicity. In Balzac, the concept of the protagonist is in place but seems unable to name and possess a single character. Is Rastignac, the obvious hero–antihero, the protagonist, or is it Père Goriot, whose life is retold through him? Or is it Vautrin, whose predictive narrative abilities seem to encompass the whole potential of Parisian life? In Balzac, social multiplicity finally comes to the centre as the centre. We are only ever amongst types: 'the kind of woman who', 'the sort of man that'; a process extending to actions, thoughts and emotions—each of them only ever one of a set that has been, and will be, endlessly repeated. Yet this centring on social multiplicity creates other instabilities. For Woloch, the type is not merely a representative of a class-fraction, *à la* Lukács. Any character's typicality is an effect of the fragmented and over-populated field in which they find themselves. Rastignac's fantastical aspirational desires make sense only in a world where competition is likely to leave his dreams unrealized.

Balzac also requires us to reconsider Woloch's account of the relations between fullness and distortion, interiority and exteriority. With persuasive originality, Woloch challenges us to think about 'flatness' as a strategy of representation which speaks to a specific historical context. This effects another of those brilliant defamiliarizations, but leaves the rounded character rather too securely in its place. Just before Vautrin is taken into custody as the arch-criminal of all criminals, his red hair—carefully concealed by dark wigs up to this point—is exposed: 'They say that redheads are very good or very bad'. Woloch mentions physiognomy a number of times, but he does not consider the place of physiognomical discourse in so many novels of this period. Madame Vauquer's comment about redheads is a typical, if crude, version of the ambivalent status that physiognomy has in Dickens, Wilkie Collins, Eliot, Gaskell and others, but its presence signifies. Physiognomy asserts a very different linkage between interior and exterior: that of continuity. Sometimes the exterior is all we need: there is no necessary effacement of the interior because the exterior maps it perfectly. Emerging out of the same anxieties about unknowable urban crowds that Woloch identifies in Dickens, physiognomy purports to offer a solution. And its absence as a discourse here points to some more general problems.

In his analysis of Austen, Woloch makes too quick an equation between individuation, as a narrative process, and the classic liberal agent, equipped with the knowledge to judge and choose. There is no account here of the textual work that the Burkean social order performs as it is inscribed in the synecdochic form of the family, although this is the order to which Austen's novels are overwhelmingly committed. Competition within the marriage market is acute, but it is not exclusively individual. One sister's foolishness and immorality taints all. Darcy, already a symbolic father to his much younger sister and his estate, must right Lydia's plight if he is to marry Elizabeth. In this sense, the Bennet family as a whole (parents included) remain a singularity. The brilliant convenience is that by pleasing herself and judging for herself, Elizabeth also provides security for the entire unit. This is even more explicit in *Emma*. The eponymous heroine is certainly self-centred, but her *Bildung* is the learning of the social responsibilities that accompany her position. Emma's individualistic caprices meddle with and, on occasion, threaten to overturn the social order and it is these she must be cured of, not just for her own sake but for 'Highbury', which is only a metonym of society in general.

The family, understood in very different terms, is also largely absent from Woloch's analysis of Dickens, and here the aporia indicates a more general problem with his method. Like Lucien Goldmann, Woloch posits a homological relation between social structures and aesthetic ones. The strength of this approach is the focus on formal narrative processes, and in this vein Woloch interestingly notices the ways in which minor characters tend to proliferate at the end of Dickens's narratives: a profusion which complicates resolution. But he also neglects the kinds of resolution— however tentative—that Dickens offers. In *Great Expectations*, it is the revelation of a set of relations which are precisely *not* perverse, unlimited and finally unknowable that completes the narrative. Molly, Magwitch and Estella, who are perhaps the most difficult characters to classify and connect, turn out to be bound by natural and nameable ties: Estella is Molly and Magwitch's long-lost daughter. These relations are certainly an effect of the distorted social world the novel maps, but they also offer a fragile alternative to the dominant vision of the novel. Magwitch's generosity to Pip is, in significant part, prompted by the loss of his daughter and he dies consoled when he learns that she still lives. Woloch's approach cannot encompass the notion of *competing* discourses within the text. The family as redemptive, a moment of respite from capitalism or industrialism (as well as highly vulnerable to these forces) is a staple of nineteenth-century novelistic discourse. This discourse cannot simply be exposed or ignored; it is another myth, which needs to be read as both true (in its real social and cultural force) and unreal.

A richer and more fully rhetorical definition of the *textual* is called for, including, first, a more precise definition of genre. This book seems to be all about genre: the novel, realism and, most consistently, the realist novel are all proposed as such. But none of these are genres in the strict sense. In

The Architext, Gérard Genette defines a genre as an intersection between a particular mode of enunciation and a particular content. Romance and the detective novel are two canonical examples, indicating not only certain types of event, but crucially, their ordering, emphasis (the discovery of the body, the many replayings of the murder scene) and the perspectives from which the events are viewed (romance's centring on feminine experience, for example). The novel is a highly successful and adaptable *institution*, its very adaptability tied to its historical emergence and development as a commodity. It is best defined as a historically specific set of publishing processes—an issue to which I will return. Its history encompasses a myriad of genres, but realism is not one of them. (On this sheer variety, see Franco Moretti's 'Graphs, Maps, Trees' in NLR 24.) Realism is a *mode* of representation, one that cuts across institutions, forms and media. It significantly, but not exclusively, shapes narrational possibilities but it does not determine a distinctive type of story (though it would seem to proscribe some). The 'realist novel' is an under-specified category in narrative terms.

Conceived as a mode, however, realism could extend the possibilities of Woloch's character-system model, for which he suggestively claims a more general validity across media. More specifically, in his conclusion, he argues that the continuities between nineteenth and twentieth-century character-space 'belie the rupture. . . so often posited between realist and modernist fiction'. This is indeed persuasive but such continuities are also part of the broader history of realism. Realism is a highly versatile and enduring mode of representation, refuelled by various avant-gardes, rather than fatally damaged. It arguably remains the dominant in most literary, 'middle-brow' and mass-market novels, and in film and TV. The constitutive dynamic that Woloch identifies between major and minor characters is central to realist modes of representation, which must gesture to the many. The plays of Beckett and Pinter are not realist in significant part because there are no minor characters. Distortion and effacement belong to a more general realist strategy whose effect is always to suggest that there is more than what has been said or told: a form of the representative that suggests a surplus (of the same order) beyond it. Contemporary realisms open up further versions of the major–minor relation. In soap opera, for example, where narrative attention is constantly redistributed amongst a relatively large group of characters, a minor character can be grown into a major one. A major character can also be temporarily minored, compressed to a typical pose and reaction, but his or her major potential only ever lies dormant, waiting to return. Further, realism intersects with the production processes of different media and institutions in a variety of ways, sometimes with surprising effects. Contemporary film and TV adaptations of branded comic superheroes are faced with the problem that, although Superman and his kind are strong protagonists, they are only minor characters: distorted to their special skills (always carefully explained) and single, special purpose of saving the world—which itself has to be maintained in recognizable realist terms. The characteristic playing-up of the superhero's realist disguise in these films and programmes is the resolution of this dilemma: Clark Kent *can* develop and change.

If realism is a mode of representation, what then of genre? Woloch does not dismiss genre-centred accounts of character, but argues that, like many other approaches, genre-based analyses can tend to jump the set of questions that character-space and system propose. Genre, and other more conventional interpretations of character (above all psychological), are for Woloch most productive within the context of these concepts. It is true that, unlike many modes of character analysis, his does not uncouple character from the narrative as a whole. But here there also seems to be a problematic prioritization of sequences or levels of analysis, suggesting an estimation of critical procedures and texts in terms of their distance from or proximity to the primary reality of the 'base'. Generic, aesthetic, thematic, psychological and ideological interpretations are so many translations (however illuminating) of the form of class relations that the narrative reconstructs. Within this context, Woloch's characterizations of the relation between text and history as *refractive* or *inflective*, although making a space for the formal work of writing, are fundamentally evasive.

But is genre really only one more interpretative possibility in the way that Woloch proposes? Central to narrative, genre governs the possibilities of character and character relations, and this opens up the *rhetorical* nature of the text, its relations with other texts and contexts, more fully. Further, genre enriches our understanding of the various ways in which interiority, or 'roundness', is represented, and of its constitutive relations with the flat. Returning to *Great Expectations*, I would foreground the centrality of gothic as a genre within the novel, not only as the shaper of a temporal order— the past repeatedly returns—but for its role in governing the processes of characterization. Pip's overwhelming by the complex social world is shaped by a distinctively gothic subjectivity. Many of his attempts to understand the world are generically Fantastic in Todorov's sense: Pip is faced with a classificatory uncertainty as to the status of the object he is perceiving. The first encounter with Miss Havisham is a classic instance. She does not only or most importantly signify 'faded youth', as Woloch suggests, but the crisis presented by the living dead (a waxwork, a clothed skeleton), and it is this gothic dynamic between perceiver and perceived that constitutes their relations. But *Great Expectations* is also in part a proto-detective novel, and for much of it Pip is a very poor detective. The complex metonymic chains that Woloch identifies, linking capital and labour, are also *clues* to the identity of

Pip's benefactor and the dubious nature of (his) wealth. One of the central genre shifts is the retuning of Pip's interiority, as his unstable Gothic subjectivity is increasingly supplanted by the certainties of forensic observation. It is he who solves the mystery of who Estella's mother is, by identifying the hereditary connexion with Molly (they share the same hands).

Conceiving character as governed by genre in this way depends on viewing texts as *intertextual*: a variation and transformation of existing texts and genres. Intertextuality is present as a concept in *The One vs the Many*, but it is not fully metabolized, foreclosing various ways in which character relations could be further developed. This seems to be a consequence of Woloch's rigid eschewal of any kind of post-structuralist thinking—a sympathetic position in certain ways. The forced growth of the marginal to absurd consequence; reading against the grain to a point of perversity; the hyperbolizing of the textual as what is always fundamentally unstable and fragmentary—all these cut against the claim of contextual specificity that such readings routinely make, leaving aside the often scanty textual evidence on which they are based. Woloch's readings take the whole text on in immensely satisfying ways, insisting on each's part in the narrative structure of the whole, and this is no small achievement when dealing with a writer such as Dickens.

But there is a price to be paid. Woloch insists too strongly on the unity of the text as an achieved (as opposed to desired) structure, and this renders him hostile in general to 'resistant' readings, whatever their goals and strategies, just as he is unwilling to see competing and irreconcilable discourses. For example, Woloch is brilliant at assessing the various modes of dispatching minor characters, for which the children's suicide note in *Jude the Obscure*, 'Done because we are too menny', might stand as metaphor. But he never considers the characters that the text cannot dispatch. What about Jackie Bast, Leonard's unpresentable working-class wife in Forster's *Howards End*? After her husband's death, she and her presumably parlous state are never mentioned. This is not the dispatch of a minor character: the novel simply cannot encompass her in its resolution. The intertextual relations between genres within a text can open up richer ways of exploring how interiority is represented and related to both exteriority and minority—as in the case of Pip's gradually discarded gothic interiority. Just as Woloch argues that the dominant protagonist constitutes subordinated minor characters, there is usually a dominant genre (or genres) within the text that will subordinate the others. The later novels of Henry James offer an interesting twist to the highly versatile gothic. In James, gothic interiority is not, as it is so often in Dickens, what has to be renounced (even as it may find a new 'host' in other children, symbolic or literal), but a mode of representing acute psychic instabilities and conflicts. In *The Wings of the Dove*, the American heiress Milly Theale has the uncanny experience of 'seeing' her friend Kate Croy as if she were looking at the absent man they jointly but secretly love, Merton Densher. Densher's spectral presence registers the conflictual subject positions that Milly occupies within this triad: as a fantasizing voyeur in a relationship she is excluded from, as the subject of her desire for Densher and, in Densher's position, as the subject of her (impossible) desire for Kate. But the gothic takes its form from its subordinated position within the genres of the novel and in particular, one of its dominants: naturalism. And James would make an interesting addition to Woloch's corpus. For in his novels, with their excessive attention to interiority, we are still only ever a moment, a circumstance, a minor character away from a social type: Isabel Archer could have been Henrietta Stackpole, Gilbert Osmond could have been Edward Rosier.

I have suggested that the novel is an institution defined by the historically specific processes of publishing. This is the other sense in which texts, genres and characters need to be understood in a fully rhetorical sense. Any genre, any text is governed by what I have elsewhere termed 'the horizon of the publishable', what it is thinkable to publish within a given historical situation. This horizon is neither a singular nor an autonomous logic defined by the 'industry'. Rather it is defined in the relations between the processes of publishing and other institutions—commercial, legal, political, educational, cultural—and, most obviously, other media. It constitutes what it is possible to write and, significantly, how it is written, marketed, edited, designed and produced. In this sense publishing always precedes writing.

Thus, returning briefly to Dickens and his minor characters, we need to situate his writing within the processes of publishing of the period and the broader horizon in which they operate. It is a truism that one of Dickens's preferred strategies for constituting characters is through dialectal and idiolectal variation and exaggeration. But what part of this is governed by the relations between publishing, other media and the institutions and practices of reading? Arguably a rather large part. It is not just that Dickens was a highly successful dramatic reader or performer, in Britain and America. The relations between stage and novel were highly synergistic at this time, with official and pirated adaptations of novels staged hot on the heels of publication. Theatrical writing was both an established model and an ambition for many novelists because it could be so lucrative. Likewise, reading aloud was a central practice within recreational and improving reading, in significant part because of patterns of literacy. Do not these contexts, only briefly sketched, go some significant way to explain the highly distinctive modes of speech of Dickens's characters (minor in particular)? These processes are not mere circumstances or enrichments, of the kind that conventional book-history canonically proposes. They are constituents of the historical horizon

REVIEW

of the publishable which *constitutes* writing. This particular variety of the written-to-be-read aloud is not a refraction of 'real' social relations: it is always already inscribed and constituted in these relations, through that horizon.

I outline these positions in criticism of *The One vs the Many*, yet in a form that is already indebted to Woloch's bold undertaking. This book insists on questions that have been skirted or marginalized, but cannot be made to go away.

Karl Marx and Friedrich Engels, *The Communist Manifesto*,
ed., Gareth Stedman Jones
Penguin: London 2002, £4.99, paperback
304 pp, 0 1404 4757 1

JACOB STEVENS

EXORCIZING THE MANIFESTO

Canonized by the Penguin Classics imprint, the latest edition of the
Communist Manifesto is dwarfed by a 185-page introduction, described by its
author as 'an excavation of the intellectual antecedents of Marxist thought'.
Serious archaeology on such a scale is to be welcomed, although the forty-
odd pages of the Manifesto may seem a slender basis from which to mount
such an exercise; and indeed, Stedman Jones here shows little interest in
the text itself. Though praising the invocation of capitalism's prodigious
revolutionizing and universalizing powers in the first section, 'Bourgeoisie
and Proletarians', he sees a descent into bathos in the second, 'Proletarians
and Communists', which advocates the overthrow of capitalist property relations, the abolition of the bourgeois family, the end of the 'exploitation of
one nation by another' and the 'radical rupture with traditional ideas'. The
third part, 'Socialist and Communist Literature', is 'arbitrary and sectarian',
while the fourth, outlining the communists' position in relation to existing
opposition parties, is 'hurriedly jotted' and 'unfinished'.

Instead, the importance of the Manifesto in Stedman Jones's reading is
rather that it epitomizes Marxism's fundamental error: the break away from
an explicit humanism towards a materialist and determinist analysis. The
structure of the argument is an inverted skeleton of Althusser's: the mistake
of Marx and Engels was to decry all former religious and ethical influences
and to deny ideas a role in history; but this departure from humanism was
fundamentally an exercise in self-deception. Their hostility to Stirner's
Romantic individualism—also pivotal for Althusser—isolated them from
these healthy currents, and they could only attempt to sneak in their normative humanist commitments via a set of increasingly elaborate evasions and

erasures. 'In the drafting of the Manifesto, any reference to these ideas . . . disappeared'; yet, as an inspiration to political action, it continued to draw, illicitly, on this ethical and religious background. Despite its secular façade, Marxism is to be categorized as an 'organized post-Christian religion'.

The substance of the case for this reading of the Manifesto is argued in the form of a genealogy, with the religious element in each current of thought brought into the foreground. Over the course of the text this method results in a slightly disorientating staccato effect, as each section brings the reader up to the point of publication in 1848, before tracking back to the next tributary. The reader is presented, therefore, with the repeated discovery of a 'new' religious lineage: the polemical effect is to discourage any chronological construction of intellectual history; including, perhaps especially, the secularizing narrative of the Manifesto itself. The traditional view that Marxism emerged out of a tripartite meeting of French socialism, German philosophy and British political economy is reworked: the religious influences within the first two, not yet exorcized by the time of the Manifesto, are deceptively cloaked by Marx and Engels in the language of social progress and political economy. The German Historical School of Law provides a fourth strand, offering a historicized conception of property regimes and examples of different forms of common ownership. The abolition of private property under communism is grounded, interestingly, in the notion of 'negative community'.

Stedman Jones traces the use of the term 'communist' to the radical French republican clubs—the *Société des Droits de l'Homme*, in particular— that emerged during the July Revolution, drawing explicitly on Jacobin and Babeuvist traditions. Faced with repression, some—such as Blanqui's *Société des Saisons*—went underground, while others became open advocates of a reworked 'communism', as an 'ostensibly peaceful and apolitical surrogate for the forbidden idea of an egalitarian republic': notably, Cabet in his *Voyage to Icaria*. German communism, in contrast, was formulated in exile, as the economic depression of the 1830s and 40s drove artisans to Paris, London, Brussels, Zurich or Geneva. In 1840 Karl Schapper, Joseph Moll and five others established the London-based German Workers' Educational Association, which would provide an important component of the Communist League that, in 1847, commissioned the Manifesto.

In the face of what he perceives as the received account, attributed to Engels—that the 'artisan communism' of the League had little influence on the Manifesto—Stedman Jones is keen to highlight the debates that took place there. He argues that all these groups were influenced by a revived Christian radicalism in 1830s France, and particularly by the works of Lamennais: 'the impact of these books on the European mainland can probably only be compared with that once made by Tom Paine in the English-speaking world'.

REVIEW

There were a series of debates on these issues within the League, partly in response to the atheist influences of Owenism and Young Hegelianism. Cabet's proposals for communist settlements were eventually rejected, as was Weitling's call, traced here to Lamennais, for violent revolution: both were deemed premature. By 1846, when the headquarters of the League moved to London, Schapper had argued for a separation of religious and political questions, and insisted, in a clear precursor to the prescriptions of the Manifesto, that 'communism should above all enable the free self-development of individuals'. As the artisans' networks splintered between Weitling, Cabet and Proudhon, the London-based leadership invited Marx and Engels to meet them in 1847 as part of an effort 'to draw into the League other elements of the Communist movement'.

The influences of Young Hegelianism on Marxist thought, discussed at length by Marx and Engels themselves, constitute perhaps the most widely explored element of their intellectual background. Stedman Jones's account carefully follows the evolution of the group, from the publications of David Strauss and Arnold Ruge on the 'rationalization' of Christianity, through Bruno Bauer's deconstruction of the historical claims of the Gospels and his expulsion from Bonn. He documents Marx's move from academia to the *Rheinische Zeitung*, and finally Marx and Engels's collective response to Feuerbach and Stirner's work. Stedman Jones is keen to stress the extent to which the teleological nature of Hegel's system—its most 'obviously vulnerable metaphysical assumption'—is retained in Marx and Engels's thinking. The concept of alienated labour, as opposed to Feuerbach's 'species being', leads to a historicization of their account of alienation and emancipation; but this historical process is argued to be 'no less purposive than that found in Hegel'—and indeed, 'scarcely less indebted to its ancestry in Protestant thought'. Within the history of property regimes and their effects there still lurked the 'true natural history of man', merely cloaked in the 'scientific and economic-sounding relationship between the forces and relations of production'.

Stedman Jones is surely overpitching his case when he describes Marx and Engels's reaction to Stirner's 1844 critique, *The Ego and Its Own*, as 'thermo-nuclear', with commensurate 'collateral damage'. Stirner had argued that Feuerbach's attempt to reclaim the attributes of God for Man did not succeed in reattributing them to human individuals, but merely shifted them to another ideal construct: the 'essence of Man'. Just like the Protestant God, this idealized notion—fundamentally derived from 'the tearing apart of Man into natural impulse and conscience'—also stood above men as their 'vocation'. Marx is explicitly identified by Stirner with the demand that 'I become a real generic Man'. His response, according to Stedman Jones, 'was to divest *all* ideas of any autonomous role whatsoever' in *The German Ideology*.

'morality, religion, metaphysics and all the rest of ideology as well as the forms of consciousness corresponding to these . . . no longer retain the semblance of independence. They have no history, no development.' (Here as elsewhere, Stedman Jones permits himself broad licence in the truncation and repunctuation of quotations; a definitive full-stop replaces Marx's semi-colon, and the famous peroration that follows: 'but men, developing their material production and their material intercourse, alter, along with this their actual world, also their thinking and the products of their thinking. It is not consciousness that determines life, but life that determines consciousness.')

Instead, political economy will be pressed in to take the place of ideology. The notion of the division of labour is improbably portrayed as a straight-forward substitute: 'as a result of his reading of *The Wealth of Nations*, Marx replaced the still somewhat abstract opposition between 'alienated labour' and Man's 'species being' by Adam Smith's conception of the development of the division of labour'. In Smith's insight, Stedman Jones's Marx sees a dynamic process that can unfold in 'antagonistic conjunction' with 'the true natural history of Man', now described as 'the development of Man's "productive forces"'. (The degree to which the concept of alienated labour might inform *Capital*'s account of capitalist exploitation is left untouched.) The image of a communist form of property that animates the Manifesto as a political goal derives, it is argued, from a combination of seventeenth-century natural law debates and the historicized conception of property relations developed by the German Historical School of Law. Marx was acquainted both through discussions with his lawyer father and through his own undergraduate studies with the challenge this School mounted to the Napoleonic codification of the absolute rights of private property, chiefly by way of a set of historical comparisons—especially Roman and Greek—that highlighted alternative forms: tribal, collective and, subsequently, state owner-ship. Stedman Jones suggests that in *The German Ideology* Marx reworked the findings of Niebuhr, Hugo and Pfister, in connection with successive stages in the division of labour.

Less convincingly, seventeenth-century natural law debates are seen as refracted through Proudhon, the Scottish conjectural historians or, more generally, 'dispersed in an array of social and political debates occasioned by the French Revolution'. Partly in order to avoid the political implications drawn by the Levellers and others from the scholastic tradition—that God had given the earth for mankind to hold in common—an account of 'nega-tive community' had been developed by Grotius and Pufendorf as a stage that preceded *any* notion of property, whether private or communal. This primeval stage was dominated by the satisfaction of needs, and a notion of rights (and hence property) was argued to have emerged once popula-tion growth necessitated the division, hence differential reward, of labour.

REVIEW

Following the work of Hont and Ignatieff, and Emma Rothschild, Stedman Jones traces the views of Grotius and Pufendorf through to Adam Smith: this is at least a plausible lineage. But to argue that their notion of 'negative community' animates Marx and Engels, with no direct textual evidence—amidst a wealth of detailed research into forms of property—would seem to contradict every word in the Manifesto and thereafter about the nature of utopian socialism. If the aim is to find intellectual forerunners for the political and economic demands made by Marx and Engels in the Manifesto, there are far stronger grounds for citing Fichte's *Closed Commercial State*, published in 1800, which advocated a wholly nationalized economy, with extensive regulation and government control of a closed paper-money supply. Although Stedman Jones footnotes a letter in which Marx says that he is grappling with Fichte, this avenue is left unexplored.

The three components that constituted Marx's conception of communism at the time of the Manifesto, Stedman Jones argues, were:

> first, an apocalyptic reading of Smith's theory of the division of labour, in which the progress of commercial society had turned towards self-destruction; second, the assumption that the modern bourgeois form of private property, like the previous forms of property discussed by the Historical School, was ephemeral; and third, the assumption that modern industry and 'the automatic system' were creating a new epoch of abundance relative to human need and comparable to, though infinitely richer than, the first primeval stage of human history.

In the years that followed, this notion would begin to disintegrate. Firstly, a mention of 'the labour time necessary for the satisfaction of absolute needs' in the *Grundrisse* is taken as a tacit admission that this would need to be allocated, reintroducing the 'government of men' in place of the 'administration of things'. Secondly, the concept of 'use value' in *Capital* was a 'direct and authentic characterization of human need concealed beneath the trafficking of the market'. A society based on use value, according to Stedman Jones, would need to be one in which the market was abolished, to be replaced by 'a rational plan worked out between the associated producers': 'Had he persisted through to the end with the concept of use value that he developed in the first and only completed volume of *Capital*, Marx would have been in danger of replacing capitalism with a pre-market form.' The last phase of Marx's life, buried in 'the intensive study of ancient, communal and pre-capitalist forms', was marked by his failure to develop a theory of modern communism, and his resulting inability to complete *Capital*. The Manifesto promise, of 'an association, in which the free development of each is the condition for the free development of all', turned out to be an 'uncashable cheque'. Implausibly, Stedman Jones imputes to Marx and Engels the view that the abolition of bourgeois property relations would necessarily involve the total abolition of the market. In light of the Manifesto's demand for 'a heavy progressive or graduated income tax'—nowhere in existence, at the time of writing—it would seem that some form of market must survive. If the Manifesto's vision of the path to a communist society can be argued to be teleological, it can only implausibly be held to harken back to a mythical Golden Age.

The overarching theme, then, of Stedman Jones's account is that communism was constituted by a normative, largely religiously inspired, vision of a future society, disguised, after Stirner's critique, in determinist, economic terminology. It is his view, as a result of this 'deception' reading, that by the time of the Manifesto the trap has been set: the combination of religious and utopian commitments and a mistaken and dogmatic determinist materialism leads directly to the 'debacle' of *Capital*. It is, of course, a reading that necessitates a refusal to take Marx and Engels at their own word throughout. There is no attempt to engage with the Manifesto's own description of the disenchanting process of capitalist development—the argument that the critique of religion, as of ethics, law, politics and the state, was now possible as never before, when:

> All fixed, fast-frozen relations, with their train of ancient and venerable prejudices and opinions are swept away, all new-formed ones become antiquated before they can ossify. All that is solid melts into air, all that is holy is profaned, and man is at last compelled to face with sober senses, his real conditions of life, and his relations with his kind.

Stedman Jones pays little attention to the manifesto as a form, both political and literary. Here, his scanting of the two final sections of the Manifesto is important. Their political role, in drawing a boundary between the world-historical force of international, revolutionary communism and its utopian competitors, is barely acknowledged; the astonishing changes in register, as the text moves between different forms of argument and addresses various audiences, remain unexamined. It is precisely the break towards actual proletarian movements—away from sacred articles of belief—that makes the Manifesto a unique document in terms of political orientation and strategy. At both of these levels—political strategy and literary technique—an important predecessor is oddly absent from Stedman Jones's genealogy: Abbé Sieyès's 'What is the Third Estate?', of January 1789: a paradigm of revolutionary Enlightenment reason. Furet captured the tone of Sieyès's pamphlets: 'violent, categorical, taut as an arrow winging to its target and piercing old society in its vital spot—privilege'. Despite the Abbé's office, the argument is entirely secular. Beginning with the question of who produces the society's wealth, he argues that the Third Estate is:

the strong and robust man who has one arm still shackled . . . What is the
Third Estate? Everything, but an everything shackled and oppressed. What
would it be without the privileged order? Everything, but an everything free
and flourishing.

Here we find clear forerunners of three crucial ideas: the universal role of
an economic class, the chains that shackle it and the ultimate goal of the
'free and flourishing' development of all; set forth in the same style that
causes Stedman Jones to regard the Manifesto as messianic. An article in
the *Rheinische Zeitung* in 1842 shows that Marx was well aware of these pamphlets; yet, though steeped in French Revolutionary ideas, Stedman Jones
neglects even to mention Sieyès. In one respect, perhaps, the pamphlets
would distort the shape of his argument: they betray a part of the Manifesto's
intellectual heritage that cannot be reduced to pseudo-religious longing,
being a product, instead, of the growing convergence of a range of debates
about economic production and political representation.

The prospect of a detailed contextualization of Marx's thought, flagged in
the introduction, evokes the approach to intellectual history of the 'Cambridge
school' associated with the work of Quentin Skinner and J. G. A. Pocock. But
in many respects Stedman Jones violates the basic canons of this kind of
textual scholarship. A disingenuous slippage too often conflates the young
Marx, or 1840s German artisans, with Leninism, Stalinism, or Soviet developmentalism. The tendentious approach to quotation, already mentioned
with respect to *The German Ideology*, suggests an over-determining agenda
rather than a disinterested excavation, and produces a picture that is both
simplified and one-sided: ideology, religion and 'forms of consciousness' are
indeed grounded in a materialist conception of forces of production and
'social forms of intercourse', but the determination is not all in one direction.
The 'reciprocal action' of civil society, the state and forms of consciousness
'on one another' is stressed, and there are two halves to the statement,
'circumstances make men just as much as men make circumstances'.

But a far greater distortion of intellectual history is produced by Stedman
Jones's determination to view *The German Ideology* as the last significant
innovation in Marx's thought, and the Manifesto as representing a point
of fundamentally arrested development. The religious legacies traced in
the various currents feeding in to Marx and Engels's positions of 1847–48
are implausibly cast forward, encompassing *Capital* and the rest of their
œuvre. A properly contextualized intellectual history would surely see these
1840s works as preliminary formulations, initial sketches of historical
materialism, with the accent on economic determinism and the rooting of
ideas in social forces. Their ultimate worth cannot be read out of the text
of the Manifesto but comes from their later elaboration and contestation

in the intra-Marxist debates they initiated. When Gramsci or Sartre explore hegemony, or Marcuse and Gorz challenge the revolutionary destiny of the proletariat, they do so in ways that retain something of historical materialism. It is unsurprising that a political strategy concerned with the oppressed would stress material constraints and opportunities, especially. after the political failure of a range of religiously inspired movements.

The Manifesto is better analysed as one milestone along a path of overlapping theoretical moves, travelling away from the religious, humanist or utopian forms of socialism that Marx and Engels openly disavow in its final sections. Stedman Jones's own description of Schapper in 1846, demanding a separation between religious and political questions—an account indebted to Christina Lattek's *Revolutionary Refugees*—would mark an early stage of this process. Political disagreements within the Young Hegelians and vital interactions with proletarian movements then fed into subsequent innovations. Stedman Jones' reading of *The German Ideology* as the last significant development would need to be substantiated by a demolition of *Capital* that hangs on more than a naturalistic interpretation of the concept of use value. It is not just that this is not done: the relevant territory is barely acknowledged. One useful and opposing view is Žižek's account, in NLR 25, of use value and exchange value as competing and irreconcilable perspectives.

Stedman Jones's organizing thesis—that Marxism is another form of religion—is, of course, one of the oldest tropes of Cold War literature, predating even the equation of communism and fascism as two sides of the totalitarian coin. During the thirties, Waldemar Gurian and Eric Voegelin argued that Marxism and Nazism caricatured the fundamental patterns of religious belief, diagnosing the resulting immanentist heresies as byproducts of secularization in a decadent world, fuelled by Enlightenment myths of social transformation. After World War Two, Jules Monnerot's *Sociology of Communism* (1949) explained that Bolshevism was a 'religious sect of world conquerors' that should be viewed as a 'twentieth-century Islam'. Raymond Aron's *Opium of the Intellectuals* (1955) offered a fully fleshedout analogy with Christianity: the 'sacred history which Marxism extracts from the penumbra of plain facts' offers a messianic role for the Party. Jacob Talmon's monumental *Origins of Totalitarian Democracy* (1952) also tracks the intellectual heritage of the October Revolution to Saint-Just and Babeuf, then casting further back to Rousseau. Robert Tucker's *Philosophy and Myth in Karl Marx* (1962) saw in the 'religion of revolution' that Marx instituted a drama of salvation derived from Augustinian traditions of medieval Christianity. For Norman Cohn, on the contrary, it was the apocalyptic beliefs of the Anabaptists and their kind, luridly illustrated in his *Pursuit of the Millennium* (1957), which provided the key to the religious fanaticism of Communists and Nazis alike. Kolakowski's *Main Currents of Marxism* (1971) laments this 'bogus form of religion' for having 'presented its eschatology as a scientific system, which religious mythologies do not purport to be'.

Many of these variants analyse political movements with a Durkheimian notion of religion: as providing a mechanism for solidarity or exclusion, or answering a psychological need for community in the face of rising individualism. Within the spectrum, however, there was always a distinction between those (Monnerot, Aron, Tucker) who regarded the verdict that Marxism was a form of religion as a self-sufficient condemnation, and those (Voegelin, Kolakowski) who wanted to preserve authentic religion as a realm of higher truth, of which Marx had merely produced a sinister caricature. Stedman Jones offers a lay version of the latter: by refusing to acknowledge the historical importance of transcendent ideals and ethical values in *The German Ideology*, Marx ended up producing an ersatz religion in the Manifesto. The movement that followed was necessarily fantastical and utopian. Although Stedman Jones avoids the pairing with Nazism, at its furthest stretch his argument seems to hold Marxist 'apocalysm' responsible for the twentieth century's world wars:

> It was not the mere fact of proletarianization that generated the wars and revolutions of the twentieth century, but the experiences of social and political upheaval, shaped and articulated through the militant and apocalyptic languages of communism or revolutionary socialism. For this reason, historians have rightly likened the passions, intransigence and extremism of twentieth-century revolutions to the religious wars of the sixteenth and seventeenth centuries.

In fact, the Revolution of October 1917 was, as Hobsbawm points out in *Age of Extremes*, a revolution against the war—'Bread, Land and Peace' was not exactly an apocalyptic slogan. In World War Two, the USSR was attacked by Nazi Germany, and Soviet resistance was largely orchestrated under the banner of Russian patriotism, in the Great Patriotic War. Hobsbawm sees World War One, not Marxism, as the source of many of the passions of the 'age of extremes'. In China, Vietnam and Cuba, nationalism was a powerful element in the mixture.

The resurrection of the political religion argument in a post-Cold War context—when, as Stedman Jones informs his readers, 'belief in the possibility or even the desirability of a future communist society has become extinct'—may seem a mere intellectual curiosity. Yet far from fading away, the notion of 'political religions', often linked to modern totalitarianisms, has rarely been more popular. Since 2000 there has even been a special journal devoted to it, *Totalitarian Movements and Political Religions*, founded by the conservative English historian of Nazism, Michael Burleigh. Included in its first number was a sympathetic interview with Robert Conquest. As

Burleigh noted with satisfaction, 'Theories of totalitarianism have rarely been incompatible with theories of political religions, and such leading exponents of the former as Raymond Aron, Karl-Dietrich Bracher, Carl Friedrich and Zbigniew Brzezinski have employed these terms almost interchangeably'. Since then Emilio Gentile, an Italian historian of fascism, has produced a full-blown volume on the subject, offering an ingenious new variant: 'Soviet Russian Shintoism'. Voegelin, Monnerot (now an ornament of Le Pen's Front National), Talmon and Cohn have all been wheeled on stage once more, and the basic thesis—that the traumas of industrialization and war led to a sacralization of the political during the twentieth century—worked out in a number of new directions. For Stanley Payne, political correctness marks a new outbreak of political religion on US university campuses.

What explains the current renaissance? In some cases, an autobiographical element, the impulse to settle accounts with a radical past, is probably involved. François Furet's *Passing of an Illusion*, demonstrating once again that Nazism and Communism were twins, is the work of an ex-Communist, just as Stedman Jones is a former sixties radical. But the more general background seems to be a concern that Marxism has not been completely purged from intellectual life, and an uneasiness that new dangers, whether in the Middle East or the West itself, may now be lurking. Certainly, once Stedman Jones has written off Marxism from *The German Ideology* on, the way is clear to enunciate a more acceptable *telos* than the overthrow of capitalism. It would be, rather, 'to set the global economic system within a more sustainable and ethically acceptable framework'. A politics, in the Manifesto's words, which requires 'that the proletariat should remain within the bounds of existing society, but should cast away all its hateful ideas concerning the bourgeoisie'.

ier
over
orists.
and the
ovements;
cinema and

VE ACCESS?

able tool for research
contains many course-
r librarian to ensure that
o the NLR Digital Archive:
y users have instant access to
line. At the moment all articles
available, with the rest to follow
ear.

to thank the Barry Amiel and Norman
t for an initial grant towards this project.

www.newleftreview.org

CPSIA information can be obtained
at www.ICGtesting.com
Printed in the USA
BVHW052339060223
658029BV00003B/51